Penguin Education

Penguin Science of Behaviour
General Editor: B. M. Foss

WITHDRAWN

Developmental Psychology
Editor: B. M. Foss

The Development of Behaviour
W. Mary Woodward

Penguin Science of Behaviour
General Editor: B. M. Foss
Professor of Psychology, Bedford College,
University of London

**Abnormal and Clinical
Psychology**
Editors: Max Hamilton
Nuffield Professor of Psychiatry
University of Leeds
Graham A. Foulds
University Department of
Psychiatry, Royal Edinburgh
Hospital

Cognitive Psychology
Editors: P. C. Dodwell
Professor of Psychology,
Queen's University at
Kingston, Ontario
Anne Treisman
Institute of Experimental
Psychology, University of
Oxford

Developmental Psychology
Editor: B. M. Foss
Professor of Psychology,
Bedford College,
University of London

Industrial Psychology
Editor: Peter B. Warr
Assistant Director of the
Medical Research Council,
Social and Applied Psychology
Unit, University of Sheffield

Method and History
Editor: W. M. O'Neil
Deputy Vice-Chancellor,
University of Sydney

Motivation and Emotion
Editors: Dalbir Bindra
Professor of Psychology,
McGill University, Montreal
Jane Stewart
Associate Professor of
Psychology, Sir George
Williams University, Montreal

Physiological Psychology
Editor: K. H. Pribram
Research Professor of
Psychology and Psychiatry,
Stanford University

Skills and Learning
Editor: Harry Kay
Professor of Psychology,
University of Sheffield

Social Psychology
Editor: Michael Argyle
Institute of Experimental
Psychology, University of
Oxford

The Development of Behaviour

W. Mary Woodward

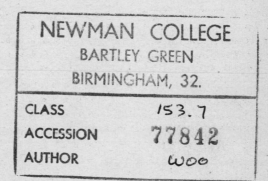
Penguin Books

Penguin Books Ltd, Harmondsworth,
Middlesex, England
Penguin Books Inc., 7110 Ambassador Road,
Baltimore, Md 21207, U.S.A.
Penguin Books Australia Ltd,
Ringwood, Victoria, Australia

First published 1971
Copyright © W. Mary Woodward, 1971

Made and printed in Great Britain by
Richard Clay (The Chaucer Press) Ltd,
Bungay, Suffolk
Set in Monotype Times

Penguin Science of Behaviour

This book is one of an ambitious project, the Penguin Science of Behaviour, which covers a very wide range of psychological inquiry. Many of the short 'unit' texts are on central teaching topics, while others deal with present theoretical and empirical work which the Editors consider to be important new contributions to psychology. We have kept in mind both the teaching divisions of psychology and also the needs of psychology at work. For readers working with children, for example, some of the units in the field of Developmental Psychology will deal with psychological techniques in testing children, other units will deal with work on cognitive growth. For academic psychologists, there will be units in well-established areas such as Cognitive Psychology, but also units which do not fall neatly under any one heading, or which are thought of as 'applied', but which nevertheless are highly relevant to psychology as a whole.

The project is published in short units for two main reasons. Firstly, a large range of short texts at inexpensive prices gives the teacher a flexibility in planning his course and recommending texts for it. Secondly, the pace at which important new work is published requires the project to be adaptable. Our plan allows a unit to be revised or a fresh unit to be added, with maximum speed and minimal cost to the reader.

Above all, for students, the different viewpoints of many authors, sometimes overlapping, sometimes in contradiction, and the range of topics Editors have selected will reveal the complexity and diversity which exist beyond the necessarily conventional headings of an introductory course.

B.M.F.

Contents

Editorial Foreword

It has been argued that a great deal of behaviour should be described in terms of 'actions' rather than 'responses' since the behaviour seems directed to a goal rather than just elicited by a stimulus. Some psychologists have considered that the directedness is controlled by a 'cognitive structure' whereas others have kept to simpler stimulus–response notions, using the mechanism of feedback to explain it. However, anyone who has watched a child developing will know that behaviour is not only directed to goals, it also becomes complex through the way it is patterned or structured, both spatially and in time sequences. It becomes increasingly difficult to provide explanations based on associationist s–r principles. This is true of a child's use of language but also of his behaviour in general, especially when trying to solve problems.

Many people interested in child development regard Piaget as the one theorist who has really attempted to come to grips with the complexity of cognitive growth, all the way from neonatal behaviour to adult thinking. There are also many psychologists who find his theory difficult to understand, difficult to interpret in terms of the activity of the nervous system and difficult to relate to simpler ideas arising from animal experiments. They may also think that, although the evidence for Piaget's 'developmental stages' is excellent, he has failed to give any convincing explanation of how a child passes from one stage to the next. (This view may arise partly from ignorance since there is such a large amount of work coming from the Geneva school.)

In the present book, Dr Woodward explores this difficult topic – the development of complex directed behaviour in the young child. She incorporates some of her own experimental work which derived from her early Piagetian experiments, but which have now developed into ingeniously simple studies of the behaviour of children solving problems. Some of this work is illuminating on the possible mechanisms which are involved in proceeding between stages of cognitive development. On the theoretical side, Dr Woodward depends partly on Piaget's formulations but she also uses other structural concepts such as the TOTE as described by Miller, Galanter and Pribram. This provides an important link with other cognitive psychologies; and since the TOTE is based on what is known about the functioning of the nervous system, especially the mechanism of feedback, it is possible to see the basis for a *rapprochement* between the approach that needs a 'cognitive structure' and that which uses stimulus–response notions.

Although the book deals with such issues, it is written in a way which makes it readable for anyone seriously interested in child development; and the frequent practical examples of child behaviour make certain that the whole thing remains firmly related to the empirical evidence. These examples could form a useful collection in their own right.

B.M.F.

Preface

The student of human development has to consider a wide variety of behaviour and mental processes, since development spans a range from the reflex to adult reasoning. The main problem is to elucidate the relation of the more complex to the more simple.

Some developmental psychologists think it is useful to examine pattern as a feature of behaviour, with a view to making qualitative distinctions; the second step is to ask questions concerning the process by which one form changes into another more complex one. This book introduces the reader to the kind of analysis that they make, distinguishing a complex behavioural sequence from a simpler one, on the grounds, for example, that it is a coordination of simpler ones or that it includes interpolated activities such as looking or comparing relations between things in the environment.

Any book is the result of discussions with many people. The contributions of those who wrestled with the early drafts of the manuscript and made detailed comments have been particularly valuable. I am very grateful to Mr F. Clough, Mrs M. Heber and Mr D. J. Middleton for their help in this way. I also wish to thank Mr R. L. Smith and Mr P. Winfrow for their help in compiling the index.

W.M.W.

1 Analysis of Behaviour

Pattern, or organization, in perception has long been recognized; attention to it as a feature of behaviour is more recent. This monograph is about the development of organized behaviour in the human individual. It is thus concerned with actions that are directed towards objects in the external environment or towards other parts of the body.

Three questions may be asked about directed behaviour. What starts it off? What controls the order in which a sequence of actions is performed? And what terminates it? The second one, the control of order, will be the main subject of discussion. The others on the conditions that start and stop the whole sequence are questions of motivation which will only be touched upon.

The developing individual continuously interacts with his environment, while at the same time maturing physiologically. The human adult has a history of many such interactions, one result of which is the formation of systems of organized past experience, which includes expectancies, beliefs and values concerning his world and himself. These influence the way he perceives and construes events, and how he deals with problems he encounters. Further, the interactions have led to the development of more and more complex means for combining past experiences in new ways; these determine the ways in which the individual gathers information about his environment and makes changes in it.

The newborn infant is equipped to make a few reflex responses to external stimulation; otherwise he makes little contact through his own actions with the world he lives in – and this occurs by chance. There are many 'free' movements of limbs in space, but these are not directed towards objects in the external environment, nor towards other parts of the body. Contact with objects occurs incidentally, when the object happens to lie in the path of the movement, or upon adult initiation. Our concern is with the development, from the behavioural repertoire of the newborn infant, of the complex skills with which adults act upon their environment – and these include the unobservable 'internal' events that we call 'thinking'.

This is the gap that has to be filled by theories of human development: from reflexes and undirected movements to logical reasoning, values and creative imagination. It is possible to start filling this gap by studying the small steps by which existing behaviour becomes modified, through learning, into a different form; alternatively the starting point may be the broad classification of the new forms that occur successively in the course of development. Ultimately a complete account of human development must do both: identify the different forms and explain the process by which one is changed into the next.

The point of view taken in this monograph is that it is first necessary to identify the main forms of behaviour and of thinking that occur successively in development. These then serve as anchoring points for the study of the detailed process of change that leads to each new form. Investigations of learning in development then become meaningful if they are carried out in order to answer specific questions concerning the process from A to B; the study of the modification of existing behaviour is then undertaken from the vantage point of *what* it results in. For example, the modification of behaviour in infancy may be investigated with a view to answering questions about the development of early forms of thinking.

Until recently the study of the modification of behaviour, or learning, has been conducted separately from the developmental perspective and from that of thinking. Mature, lower animals have mainly been used as subjects. In 1949 Hebb pointed out that much learning has already taken place in mature animals and he argued that learning in early infancy has different features from that of maturity. This led to much

research on early experience and its relation to later development, and introduced new concepts such as 'perceptual
learning'.

The reason for the separation of the study of learning
from that of thinking is historical. The early behaviourists
considered that thinking was not a proper subject for scientific
investigation. The early Gestalt psychologists, who did study
thinking, were not interested in how the past experience that is
utilized in a solution has been acquired. Thus studies in either
tradition were not likely to ask how thinking developed from
simple sensorimotor learning in the course of development.
Hebb (1949) further made the point that principles derived
from the investigation of lower animals are not likely to
elucidate the problem of human thinking and that the failure
of modern psychology to come to grips with this problem was
its greatest weakness. Since then theoretical models based on
principles of conditioning have been proposed concerning
how mediating processes such as thinking might come about;
but again these have not been related to the emergence of
such processes in children during their second year.

Piaget, in Geneva, accepting neither behaviourist nor
Gestalt principles, has, for more than forty years, been asking
questions about the development of thinking from sensorimotor behaviour and about the development of more complex
processes of thinking from simpler forms. Until recently there
was a lag of fifteen years or more between the publication and
translation of his books and it is only in the last few years that
textbooks on human development written in English have
included accounts of the more recent Genevan work and of
Piaget's invaluable observations of his own children in
infancy.

As a consequence of these conceptual and linguistic barriers,
it is common, in books on human development, for a discussion of learning to occur in one chapter and for the 'higher
processes' of remembering and thinking to be dealt with in
another, with no questions asked about how one develops into
the other – nor indeed about how the higher processes become
more complex.

These questions lead us to consider the process by which early behavioural sequences become more highly organized and how they give rise to 'higher processes' which in turn organize behaviour at yet higher levels. In order to do this, it is necessary first to discuss what behaviour it is relevant to examine and what point of view is being adopted about the relation of thinking to action. Further preliminary questions concern how detailed a description of behaviour is required and what unit of analysis is being used.

Sensorimotor behaviour

What behaviour in infancy is it useful to examine? The child in his first year performs a variety of different kinds of actions. He rolls from side to side, for instance, pulls himself to a sitting position, steps when held upright and moves about by some means or other. He also looks at the people and objects around him and performs such actions as shaking rattles, banging one object upon another, putting an object in another. The former kind of behaviour, and many others, we shall neglect, while the latter kind will be examined in detail. Why? The assumption of the upright posture and the process leading to it might be thought to be more important for human development than 'playing' with rattles and other toys.

The answer to this is that locomotion is a matter of balance and the coordination of movements of different parts of the body, without necessarily involving external objects. The elucidation of the questions posed above has to be sought in the study of behaviour that is directed towards objects in the external environment; movements of different parts of the body and coordinations between them are of interest only if they play a part in the development of behaviour that is so directed. Some of these coordinations are relevant, as when the child looks at his own hand.

The objects towards which behaviour is directed are sources of stimulation for the external receptors subserving vision, hearing and touch. Such directed behaviour is often a matter of manipulating objects and producing events from them; but it also includes looking and listening without performing any action upon the object concerned, or holding an object in the hand without moving it. A point to be stressed is that holding the head still in looking at something or holding an object in the hand or mouth are actions, just as much as moving an object. When there is overt behaviour, the motor component is observable. But if there is no movement to be seen, this does not necessarily imply there is no muscle innervation; there may be a small change which may be detected by the use of appropriate instruments. A 'holding' action, such as looking, involves innervation of the muscles of the neck, in order to hold the head still; muscles in the hand are similarly used when an object is held. Moreover, eye and ear muscles are being innervated in visual and auditory perception. For this reason it is becoming common to speak of looking and listening, as well as of visual and auditory perception. Perception is thus conceived of as an active response of the subject, not only as a subjective experience – a conception which gets rid of some of the troublesome problems in the formulation of theories about how thinking and other complex processes are developed from sensorimotor sequences.

A further point is that receptors in the muscles are stimulated in movement and in holding actions. This has been termed 'kinaesthetic feedback'.

To draw attention to the motor component in perception and to the sensory component in movement does not mean that the distinction between sensory and motor activities is blurred. There are, however, different relations between sensory and motor components in different activities; these have to be specified and appropriate terms used for them.

Three kinds of 'activity' may be distinguished. The conventional distinction between 'motor' and 'sensorimotor' behaviour turns on whether or not movements are directed towards an object or sound that is a source of sensory input for the external receptors. Following this usage, the term 'motor activity' will be reserved for the free movement of limbs in space, including locomotion of the whole body when no course is being steered towards an objective. This involves only a relation between movement and kinaesthetic input into the receptors of the muscles that are innervated. Similarly the term 'perception' will only be used when the movements involved are those of the muscles in sense organs. The term 'sensorimotor' (or perpetual-motor) will be used for behavioural sequences that consist of directed actions and input into the external receptors from the object towards which (or away from which) the action is directed.

Grasping an object that is looked at is sometimes, through insufficient analysis, classed as motor behaviour in the sense defined above, along with locomotion. Contrast locomotion when no course is being steered and when there are no obstacles to dodge with grasping a visually perceived object. The locomotion occurs without reference to any external object. Grasping requires that the individual brings his hand, from the position in space where it is, to another position in space where the object is situated, while continuing to look at the object. This, then, is coordinated visuomotor behaviour with sensory input into the visual receptors and directed action towards the stimulating object, not only a movement and kinaesthetic feedback.

It is this sensorimotor behaviour that is the subject of this monograph, which will not deal with the development of perception or motor activities alone.

The reason for selecting directed actions for analysis is that behaviour is modified through interactions with the external environment. When the child performs an action that produces an event (such as shaking a rattle and producing a sound), we are interested in whether he hears the sound. Moreover we wish to distinguish his hearing the sound, as an isolated event, from his connecting it with his action and with the object concerned. In the latter case we may speak of auditory feedback, as we may of visual feedback when the event produced is a movement that the child looks at. When such sensory feedback leads to a continuation or modification of the action, there is interaction, a sequence of inputs and movements. Moreover, when the behaviour is so modified, or occurs again in the same kind of stimulus situation, learning has taken place. When 'thinking' occurs, it may also be regarded as part of an organism–environment interaction, though it has a less direct relation to the sensory input.

Thinking and action

What is being included under the heading of 'thinking'? Hebb (1966) has made a useful distinction between 'sense-dominated' behaviour and behaviour which is such that a 'central mediating process' may be inferred; thinking is an instance of the latter. By sense-dominated behaviour, Hebb means reflex behaviour that is elicited by the 'natural' stimulus, or behaviour that is elicited by a stimulus event with which it has become associated through a process of learning, when the event is a condition for the subsequent performance of the action. In both cases the response occurs while the stimulus event is still present. This is contrasted with behaviour that occurs in relation to a stimulus event, when that stimulus event has ceased, as when there is a delay between the end of the stimulation and the performance of the action. The assumption is that some neural activity holds the excitation produced by the sensory event after the sensory receptors are no longer stimulated. The simplest example is the 'delayed reaction'. This is typically demonstrated when the subject is shown an object which is then hidden under one of three covers and response is prevented for varying intervals of time. If the subject removes the correct cover more often than would be expected by chance, postural cues to the position having been eliminated, some explanation is required of the 'holding' of the object and its position in the interval. (Some textbooks use the term 'symbolic processes' for the delayed reaction, remembering of verbal material, imagery and thinking.)

Thinking is a more complex example of a central mediating process, when the subject does more than 'hold' or remember previous events; he transforms them in some way, as when he speaks the number 10, upon hearing the numbers 6 and 4. The presentation of these two numbers can also, of course, under certain conditions, produce the answer of 2 or 24, depending on whether the additional stimulus event given with them was add, subtract, etc. Moreover, these different 'responses' cannot be explained by postulating that '10' has been learned as a response to 'add 6 and 4', and so on for the other instances, since the presentation of any two numbers can produce from subjects answers that are consistent with the operations of adding, multiplying and so forth. However, the instruction 'add' at the beginning of a list is sufficient for each pair of numbers to be added. In this case it is postulated that a process for operating upon certain kinds of input has been retrieved from the memory store. Such an operation would not be applied, for instance, if the input were words and not numbers. But again the same word elicits different responses under different conditions. The word 'horse' for instance may, under certain conditions, evoke the response of 'animal' or 'mammal'; in others it may elicit 'foal' or 'cow' or 'cart' or 'racc'. In an experiment the class of response that is required is indicated to the subjects. But in everyday life, people select their own instructions or appropriate class of word for the situation. In other words, one central mediating process triggers off another. This occurs, for instance, when an individual combines two or more segments of previous experience that he has never before combined. The segments of experience may be learned behavioural sequences which, when combined in a certain order, solve a problem, or they may be inferences drawn about relations between observed events, as in reasoning, or imaginative reconstruction of previous events, as in daydreaming.

When long sequences of thinking occur, the link with previous experience and with a subsequent action may seem to be remote. It may seem justified to study thinking as an autonomous process, unrelated to action and the environment. The point of view adopted in this monograph is that 'thinking' cannot be discussed separately from action and that neither can it be considered apart from the environmental situation with which both are connected. Further, it is suggested that a process of thinking is always related to some external situation; even if the individual is not in the situation, he can remember it and reflect upon it. This also implies that a process of thinking results in action at some point – or in a state of indecision about alternative courses of action.

If processes of thinking are treated in isolation from the context of the situation to which they are related and from the ensuing action, misleading formulations may result. Humphrey (1951) made this point in a discussion of the work of the Wurzburg group, who were the first to tackle the experimental study of thinking. While acknowledging its undoubted contribution, he pointed out that the problems raised by the theoretical framework within which it formulated its views are an example of 'what happens when "thought" is analytically divorced from its context of action' (p. 30). Writing about psychological formulations made some fifty years later, Brunswik (1957) made the same statement about the organism and its environment, adding that psychology had tended to forget that it is a science of organism–environment interaction and had virtually become a science of the organism. This comment was made in the context of a discussion of the perception of space in adults, though it is equally applicable to the study of human development.

The need to consider organism–environment interaction has been recognized in the extensive study of learning, of relations between 'stimuli' and 'responses'. Both stimulus situations and responses, however, vary considerably in complexity. Behavioural sequences are often referred to as 'responses' without further analysis. This does not particularly matter if the aim is to investigate the conditions that lead to an increase or decrease in the frequency of the performance of a given item of existing behaviour; but it does matter when the focus of interest is in progressive changes in behaviour. 'R' becomes increasingly complex during development. Accordingly questions have to be asked about whether behaviour of a given complexity consists of coordinations of simpler behavioural sequences or is a modification of one; other questions concern the prior learning that is necessary for the acquisition of the more complex sequences. It has already been pointed out that directed behavioural sequences are alternations of sensory input and action. Both these, and the stimulus situations that give rise to input, require detailed description and analysis.

The description and analysis of behaviour

We will consider first what is involved in the description of behavioural sequences. Even behaviour that might be thought to qualify for description as a simple 'response' turns out, on analysis, to be complex – and this draws attention to how extremely complex is adult human behaviour.

Consider, for example, the behaviour of shaking a rattle, and similar 'responses' such as picking up an object and putting it down somewhere else.

These 'responses' are relatively complex sequences of action. For a start all involve bringing the hand from the position in space where it is to another position in space where there is the object that is looked at. The infant cannot bring his hands to grasp an object that he sees for several months after birth. Thus even this preliminary part of the 'response' is more complex than that which occurs early in development for – as we shall see in chapter 2 – it is a sequence of coordinations from simpler 'responses'. On further analysis it is a matter of responding to a visual stimulus object with a movement of the hand – and not of the mouth or of a leg – and then moving the hand towards the seen object – not shaking it in the air or scratching the table with it – opening the hand if it is closed and closing it round the object. While these actions are performed the head has to be kept in the correct position for continued visual fixation of the object. The subsequent actions are lifting and shaking the rattle and repeating the shaking action. The apparently simple action of picking up a rattle and shaking it is thus a sequence of five actions: moving the hand towards the seen object, opening the hand, closing it around the object, lifting it and shaking it. The precise performance of the grasping part of the sequence (bringing the hand to rest at the appropriate place) presupposes that the child has learned to bring his hand movements under control and that he has learned to open his hand to accommodate to differently shaped objects.

The shaking part of these actions has so far been described as one action – that of 'shaking'. Miller, Galanter and Pribram (1960) have, however, pointed out that even a simple action such as shaking consists of two actions: lifting and a downward movement through space. The example they use is the action of hammering a nail into wood; hammering consists of lifting and striking. The preliminary action of bringing the hand to an object has already been analysed into several smaller component actions. Miller, Galanter and Pribram further point out that each of these smaller components may be further analysed in terms of the muscle groups that are involved. If analysis of such apparently simple behaviour reveals such complexity, how complex is the behaviour of driving a car, of responding to 10 – 6 with 4, of constructing a three-dimensional model of a village, of hitting a moving tennis ball with a racket – or the moon with a spaceship?

Miller, Galanter and Pribram maintained that behaviour is organized simultaneously at several levels of complexity and that a full description of behaviour includes all levels; to select one may be misleading. We will return to this point and its implications for the description of behaviour at various periods of development when we have examined more complex behaviour than shaking a rattle, such as placing objects in certain spatial relations to one another.

Let us examine the behaviour of a child who has a few cubes of wood from which he builds a 'tower'. In each successive placement after the first, the cube has to be brought to the position in space where the tower is, held above it and placed on it. This requires visual and motor coordination. If the cube is then adjusted so that its sides are flush with those of the previous one, further alternations of actions and visual feedback are necessary. But what is happening when the child turns the cube into the correct position for aligning it with the others as he approaches the tower and places it flush with the others in one move? In this case we must infer that the visuomotor sequence involved in aligning is being conducted *while* the cube is being moved through space towards the tower. An action that involves placing two objects into a fairly complex spatial relation is thus 'arranged' before it is performed. There is something different here from the modification of subsequent behaviour on the basis of feedback of the result of the previous action.

Consider now the behaviour of placing a group of objects into different spatial relations with one another from aligning upwards. Suppose that each of a group of nine objects, given in a scattered arrangement as in diagram a of Figure 1, is picked up and put down somewhere else, one at a time. These nine actions of putting an object somewhere else may be performed in such a way that the objects are treated in isolation from one another, or the actions may relate them. If each object in a scattered group is picked up and moved to a different position without regard to the position of any of the others – or to any other object – the end result will be a scattered group as before. If, on the other hand, the second is placed near the first, the third near the first two, the fourth near these, and so on, the group of objects has been changed, from a scattered array to one that is close together. This is illustrated in Figure 1.

Diagram a shows the objects before they are moved. When

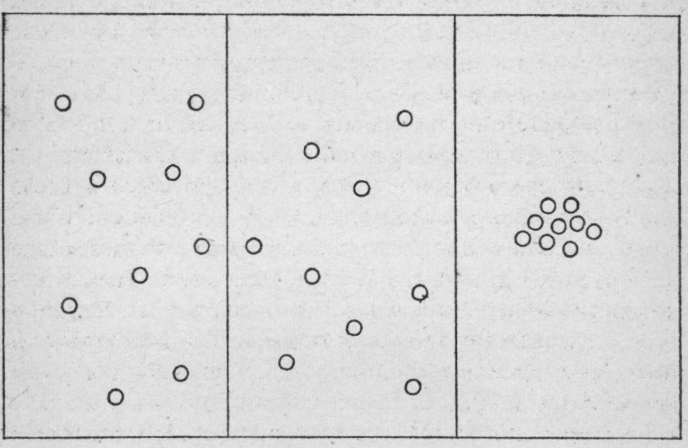

a   b   c

Figure 1

placed as in diagram b, each has been moved to a different position, but still in a scattered arrangement. In diagram c the objects have been put near together and their spatial relations have been changed. In the first case the action that is repeated is picking up and putting down an object; in the second it is picking up and putting down an object near others. When scattered objects are moved and placed in another scattered group (as when a child is told to put his toys away and he merely transports each somewhere else), there is nothing to terminate the sequence of actions – except perhaps 'boredom', whatever that means. When a different spatial arrangement such as a group close together is made, the sequence has an obvious terminating point, when no objects are apart from the rest.

Consider now the operations involved in moving a collection of objects, scattered as in diagram a of Figure 1, into the positions illustrated in Figure 2.

To achieve the result in diagram a of Figure 2, it is necessary not only to put each object near the others but to place each alongside the others; an additional spatial relation of alignment is involved. The result in diagram b requires that two more spatial relations be taken into account when the objects are positioned. These are leaving a space between the objects and placing them in the same orientation. Finally, to obtain the result in diagram c, alignments and spacing in two directions have to be achieved and with the distances approaching equality. The distance between two of the objects (e.g. numbers 1 and 2) has to be judged and repeated when three others are placed (numbers 3, 4 and 7), and the same alignment and orientation has to be maintained. The remaining four have to be simultaneously aligned with others in two directions. To make a regular pattern, such as that in diagram c, from a scattered arrangement, thus requires that several spatial relations are taken into account when the objects are positioned.

Bartlett (1958), who conceived of thinking as a high-level skill, drew attention to a finding from the study of perceptual-motor skills: halts occurred in the course of a movement when objects were being picked up and put down in assigned places. It was mentioned earlier that an object could be positioned in relation to others in one move or by several successive adjustments. This is the case, too, when objects are placed in arrangements such as those shown in Figure 2. In a sequence of successive adjustments a subsequent action is guided by the perceived outcome of a previous one; in placement in one move the action is guided by a prior perceptual and analytical process. We must thus postulate some process in the organism that organizes a behavioural sequence before its performance.

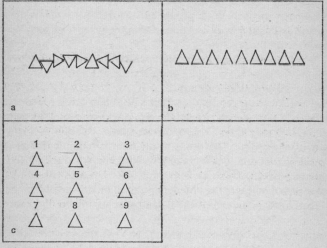

Figure 2

In other instances the postulated central process is more complex than this. Examine the behaviour of copying the pattern in diagram c of Figure 2 while aiming to make the distances and alignments more equal than can be achieved by perceptual judgements. For this a measuring instrument is required. Piaget, Inhelder and Szeminska (1960) have proposed that measurement of length requires making a logical inference of the following sort: given that A = B and B = C, then A = C when B is the measuring instrument (or a unit of it) and A and C are the two lengths measured with it. This introduces something that might be termed 'logical reasoning'. If a scale model or diagram is made of an actual object or of a section of the earth, the operations of proportion are added to those of measurement. When central processing of this kind enters into behaviour, we are beginning to close the gap between the reflexes and undirected movements of the neonate and the logical reasoning of the adult – or rather to map points that have long gaps in between.

These examples are sufficient to illustrate the points that behaviour varies in complexity in the course of development and that correct inferences concerning the process that guides the behaviour depend upon observations of the relevant behaviour having been made. At what level, then, are these various kinds of behaviour and postulated central processes to be described? We return to the statement of Miller, Galanter and Pribram (1960) that behaviour is organized at several levels of complexity and takes place simultaneously on all of them. Their main point is that 'configuration is just as important a property of behavior as it is of perception' – though it has received much less attention. They maintain that any behaviour may be analysed into smaller and smaller segments until the level of the muscle groups that are innervated in turn is reached. For example, a large or 'molar', segment of behaviour X, consists of smaller parts (e.g. A and B) and these in turn consist of yet smaller parts (e.g. A consists of a and b, and B consists of c, d and e) and so on. Their illustrative example that hammering consists of two component parts, lifting and striking, has already been mentioned. The organization is thus hierarchical. The segments at the lowest level are grouped into larger ones of the next level, these into yet larger ones at the next level, and so on. The final top level can be a very long sequence of behaviour, such as building a tool shed or studying for a degree. The hierarchical structure of behaviour may be represented diagrammatically in various ways, for example, as a 'tree structure'.

Miller, Galanter and Pribram draw attention to the fact that the practice of selecting for description only one level, at a level of larger or smaller segments, may miss some features of the behaviour, particularly its configurational properties; and it may even be misleading. If the sequence of muscle movements, or the small segments of behaviour, were described at the level of a b c d e, the ways in which they are grouped would be lost; the description of the grouping at higher levels is necessary, since different groupings, e.g. (ab) (cde) and (abc) (de) may describe different behaviour. They point out that this is most clearly illustrated with human verbal behaviour. The sentence 'They are cooking apples' can mean either '(They are) (cooking apples)' or '(They) (are

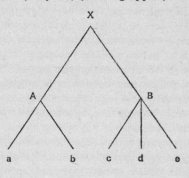

Figure 3

cooking) (apples)', and which it is is made clear only at the higher level grouping into phrases; lists of phonemes (the smallest units of speech) or of morphemes (the smallest meaningful units) would not indicate which meaning was intended.

Miller, Galanter and Pribram add that such complete descriptions of behaviour are rarely made by psychologists and that they have been more often made by linguists with regard to language and by ethologists with regard to the behaviour of lower animals. Further, when such descriptions are made, 'it is quite obvious that the behavior is organized simultaneously at several levels of complexity' (Miller, Galanter and Pribram, 1960, p. 15) so that one may speak of 'the hierarchical organization of behavior'.

The analysis of behaviour in this way begins to deal with the problem of the level at which to describe behaviour at different periods in development. Behaviour early in development has very few levels, but in adolescence many. In between there are progressively more levels. The number of levels might, therefore, be a means for distinguishing different forms of behaviour – once the problem of identifying criteria for a new level has been overcome. A possible criterion of a new level is when two existing behavioural sequences are coordinated; another is the modification of existing behaviour. Description of behaviour (e.g. at level C) thus needs to be detailed in terms of the behavioural sequences of at least the previous level (B) from which it is developed. When it in turn is incorporated in yet more complex behaviour (level D), detailed description at level B may then be dropped. For example, the behaviour of grasping an object that is looked at needs to be analysed and described in at least the detail given earlier in this chapter. This was bringing the hand to the position in space occupied by the object that is looked at, while holding the head still and fixating the object, opening the hand and closing it round the object. Given this description, it is then necessary to examine the development of the visual control of hand movements, of the eliciting of hand movements upon visual contact with an object, of opening and closing the fist, of retaining objects in the hand, etc. Once grasping seen objects has developed, it can be referred to at the highest level, as grasping objects on sight – remembering that it consists of the coordination of behavioural sequences with fewer levels. In considering the early development of concepts of space, a detailed description is necessary of the way objects are placed in relation to one another, but the level of grasping, lifting, moving the object through space and releasing it may be omitted. Similarly, the details of the sequence of actions of placing objects in certain positions can be neglected when we elicit behaviour from the child in order to find out whether he understands the principles of measurement and whether he can relate objects to an abstracted spatial framework. These can be described as 'measuring' or 'mapping' or 'making a scale model'.

The unit of analysis

Having settled the level at which behaviour is being described, the next question to be dealt with concerns the unit of analysis that is appropriate to the subject matter. The traditional one is the s–r unit. The increasing complexity of 'responses' during development has already been illustrated. The examples given also illustrate the increasing· complexity of the 'stimulus situations' to which the behaviour is related: from a single object to an increasingly complex matrix of spatial relations among objects. A 'stimulus' may equally be a single property of an object, such as its colour, or a set of objects that have several attributes on which they vary, or are alike, such as colour, size, form and pattern. On the basis of these regularities people can make a classification of the material – a complex 'response' not found in early childhood. Complexity in 'stimulus situation' and 'response' thus go hand in hand.

When an action upon an object produces an event from it, there are two sources of input, the object and the outcome. In complex sequences such as placing objects in patterns, as in Figure 2, or making a scale diagram or model, there are several 'outcomes'; what they are depends on the level of behaviour that is considered. One is the outcome at the highest level of analysis, the completion of the scale model or the spatial pattern; another is the outcome of more specific actions in the sequence such as measuring or seeing the altered arrangement when an object is placed in certain relations to others; at another level the outcome is seeing an object on a surface after the action of releasing it; at another lower level, the outcome is kinaesthetic feedback.

Miller, Galanter and Pribram (1960) have proposed a unit of analysis that can take account of these various levels of action and outcome all at once. This follows from their analysis of behaviour as organized at several levels of complexity. It is based on the concept of the feedback loop, or self-regulatory mechanism; this concept is adopted from engineering. The simplest example is a thermostat, which operates to effect a decrease or increase in heat within certain limits. Applied to human behaviour, an action is regulated by feedback of the outcome of the previous action. Reinforcement is a particular kind of feedback, in certain situations, though sensory feedback is not identical with reinforcement. (See Annett, 1969, in this series, for a discussion of feedback and human behaviour and its relation to reinforcement.) The unit is termed a TOTE by Miller, Galanter and Pribram, the first three letters symbolizing the feedback loop, and the last the termination of the sequence. The T stands for test phase and the O for operate phase, and behaviour alternates between them (TOT), until the conditions of the test are satisfied, whereupon the sequence is terminated. The sequence is initiated by a state of incongruity between, for example, a state of the organism and a state of affairs in the environment. The sequence of testing and operating continues until there is congruity.

The illustrative example used by Miller, Galanter and Pribram is that referred to earlier – hammering a nail into wood. The two component actions of lifting and striking constitute the operate phase. The action of striking is followed by visual feedback of its outcome concerning the position of the nail in relation to the wood. Different outcomes are the conditions for the repetition or termination of the behaviour of hammering. If the nail sticks up, hammering is repeated; if it is flush with the wood, that particular kind of behaviour is terminated. The test in this case is 'Is the nail flush with the wood?' The satisfaction of the requirements of the test is the condition for the termination of the action and the cessation of the action is expressed by E for exit. The unit is thus a TOTE.

The language of computer programming is used in this formulation. The satisfaction of the conditions of the test is a stop-rule for action, as it is in a computer program for terminating a certain kind of operation that is being executed. 'Tests' are similarly written into computer programming and the 'program' or set of instructions concerning the sequence of operations, which is written in the relevant language for the computer, can also be depicted as a 'flow chart'. Similarly, Miller, Galanter and Pribram illustrate their concept of the TOTE unit by a flow chart as in Figure 4.

Since there is also kinaesthetic feedback when there is

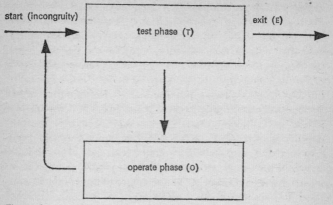

Figure 4

movement of a limb, a more detailed flow chart for the activity of hammering a nail into wood would require the expansion of the operate phase to show the order of the performance of the component actions of lifting and striking, together with the test phases concerning the position of the hammer (up or down) after each movement (kinaesthetic feedback). Each component action of lifting and striking is thus a TOTE. In this case the test for terminating the sequence ('Is the nail flush with the wood?') becomes a major test which is performed after each cycle of the two TOTEs in the lifting and striking sequence. Miller, Galanter and Pribram term this a 'proto-test'; the operate phase which forms the whole TOTE consists of the two TOTEs of the two component actions.

Behaviour at several levels of complexity can thus be catered for by this concept: the operate phases at a higher level can be expanded into further TOTE units for the lower levels. The proto-test is the one that governs the termination of the whole sequence and the outcomes of other tests determine whether the smaller segments of behaviour are repeated or are terminated. This system can include central events such as thinking; the operate phases need not be overt actions.

For example, a task, described in chapter 6, of finding out

what determines the flexibility of rods requires a succession of comparisons of the two rods that are equal in all respects but one. The rods given vary in four ways (length, thickness, etc.) and the weight to be placed on the tip also varies. Thus before every overt action of taking two rods to compare, five TOTES without overt action, except looking, are made, involving four judgements of equality and one of difference which are made before two rods are selected. After this the action is performed that requires another test: 'Do they bend the same amount?' This is only one of a succession of such comparisons. Unless a stop-rule is built into the system, the comparisons would go on. The way the subject ensures that he stops when he has examined each variable would, with these concepts, be catered for with a higher level test such as 'Are there any more left?' (This also requires that he remembers those that he has compared and what the result was.) The next phase then consists of operations of judgement without overt action and their test phases involved in examining the relations between the results obtained from the comparisons and drawing a conclusion from them.

In the examples of behaviour that have been discussed earlier, the proto-test would be 'Are all the buildings represented in the scale model?' and 'Have all the objects been moved somewhere else?' or 'Are there any more left?' Notice, however, that the end-result in diagram b of Figure 1 has no stop-rule given by the nature of the 'task' that the individual has undertaken. The behaviour of picking up an object and putting it down could continue indefinitely, since there is no final arrangement towards which the actions are directed. Since it does cease, the stop-rule is of a different kind: the arrival of a person who diverts 'attention', seeing another toy that does so or some state of the organism which may loosely be described as 'boredom' or 'satiation', the physiology of which has not been precisely elucidated.

For this reason the flow chart of the behaviour of shaking a rattle and banging a toy on a table differ from that of hammering a nail into wood, although the operate phases of all consist of the two actions of upward and downward movements.

The feedback from shaking a rattle and banging a toy on a table is a sound; that the toy in the latter case is brought into contact with another object is irrelevant. In hammering, the effect of the action of the hammer upon the relation of two other objects is the whole point of the exercise. When the relation of the two objects is that the head of the nail is flush with the wood, the conditions of the test are satisfied and the activity ceases; testing involves the interpolated action of looking. The stop-rule for the two behaviours of the infant must again be sought in some other condition. Thus, in applying these concepts to the analysis of behaviour in development, we shall have to ask about changes in conditions for stop-rules, as well as in the number of levels in the behaviour.

The question of an organizing principle

Behaviour is not only initiated and terminated; the actions and central operations in a sequence occur in a certain order. In s–r analyses it is assumed that the performance of a learned sequence of different actions occurs as a 'chain-reaction', each item being a cue for the next one. Postulated central mediating processes, in the form of implicit stimuli and responses, are derived from actual stimuli and responses, and relations between them are assumed to be governed by the same principles that have been found to govern relations between external stimuli and responses. A sequence of mediating processes is thus conceived of as chained, each giving rise to the next.

Miller, Galanter and Pribram (1960), on the other hand, maintain that the central process that controls the order in which actions and central operations occur is hierarchical. They point out that a computer cannot provide the answer to the problem fed into it, draw what is relevant from its stores and process the data, unless it is given instructions in the form of a program. Consequently they argue that man's behaviour equally cannot be explained without postulating a set of instructions which guide the sequence of actions and processes involved in gathering, retrieving and transforming data. They term this a plan which is 'any hierarchical process in the organism that can control the order in which a sequence of operations is to be performed'. The postulate of a hierarchical structure for the organizing and coordinating process is derived from their analysis of behaviour. Although the sequence of events can be described as a temporal sequence, each succeeding the other, it is maintained that the organizing is achieved from the higher levels to the lower. If a tree diagram were made of the behaviour of constructing a scale model of a group of buildings, the top stalk at the top of the tree would represent the level described as making a scale model of buildings a, b, c, d, etc. The lower level actions of assembling the necessary material and of the operations of measuring and calculating proportions are selected and ordered in accordance with the envisaged outcome of the completed model.

Children cannot envisage the outcome of sequences of actions they have never performed in that order until a certain point in development. Hence, although the concept of the feedback loop and the analysis of behaviour into several levels may usefully be applied all through development, the question of whether the concept of plan is appropriate for all periods of development is a matter for discussion. One possibility is that plan is a useful concept to apply to behaviour after a certain point in development but not before it; such a point might be, for example, when a number of different segments of one level are strung together into a sequence, making a different level.

The analysis of the environment

Having discussed the complexity of behaviour at some length, the final introductory point to be considered is the specification of the environment upon which actions are performed, and the learning situations that the child is presented with. In a general way, the environment may be described as consisting of objects in three-dimensional space and events that occur in time. The objects have features such as variations in shape, colour, size, pattern, texture, etc., by which they may be discriminated. The spatial relations may also vary: some touch one another, others are at varying distances apart. From the viewpoint of an observer, some are above or below others – to the left or the right of, or in front of or behind others. Events that occur for a certain duration that may be perceived are sounds, movements of objects, splashes, etc. These, too, vary in certain ways, such as pitch and intensity. Some of the events that are perceived by an individual are produced by actions of his, and some not.

Many objects that are sources of visual stimulation for the infant are the same from day to day; the human face is a frequently recurring object as are feeding bottles, the ends of the cot and pram, toys, the permanent features of rooms. The same kinds of sounds recur, too, and in a regular manner in the presence of certain kinds of objects. Such recurrent regularities thus afford the opportunity for the child to recognize objects and sounds that he has seen and heard before.

Piaget (1953, 1955) has, however, drawn attention to the fact that the learning situations presented by his environment to the infant involve more than the discrimination and recognition of objects. When the child turns his head, he sees different objects. Does he learn that a movement of his head is followed by the outcome of the appearance of objects in his visual field? If so, how does he sort out when a change in his visual field is due to the movements of the objects themselves and when it is the outcome of his own movement? A further complication is that not all objects are stationary: people move about and they move objects which may also move when a wind blows. By moving his head and eyes the infant can keep the moving object in view, as he can by holding his head and eyes still when the object is stationary. Does he learn that movement of his head and eyes retains the visual object? If so, how does he learn when objects are moving and when they are still?

Further, some sounds and movements occur as the result of his actions upon objects, and others do not. How does the child learn to distinguish between events that are produced by his actions and those that merely occur at the same time as a movement he performs?

Some movements keep the same objects in the visual field,

but produce a change in the perceived spatial relations of the objects: some overlap others more or less, some become masked by others. On the other hand, such changes can be produced by movements of the objects. This presents another problem. A further one is whether the object that goes out of the perceptual field is the one that reappears some time later. In addition there is always a side of an object that cannot be seen. When small objects are held and turned round, that side comes into view, while the one that was in view disappears. How does the child learn that these successive perceptions are of the same object and that large objects that he cannot move have another side that he cannot see?

A world of objects, distributed in three-dimensional space, that can be looked at and touched, and of sounds that can be heard, thus presents the infant with a number of problems.

Some of these 'objects' are people. The implications of this feature of the child's environment need to be noted. In the first place, the child himself is another object in space and his actions take place in space through time; he is thereby an object and a source of sound and movement that can be perceived by other people. Secondly, the actions of people upon objects and upon other people are further complex events which the child can observe – and imitate. Thirdly, most human sounds are speech, and communication *about* objects can take place between child and adults through the medium of language. Finally, adults do not merely perceive differences in the colour, size, shape, etc. of objects and recognize some as similar to others; they also group objects by their similarity in *some* of their features – they form class concepts and classify. They also rank objects and events in order of magnitude, enumerate and perform further operations on the numbers. Moreover, they do not merely perceive the spatial relations among objects, of distance, position, etc.; they relate the objects within an abstracted coordinate system and they construct models and make drawings. Further, they investigate events that are unexpected or unusual. Thus, the child lives not only in a physical world of objects and events, but one in which this physical environment is operated upon by the people around him, both in the form of overt actions and of 'thinking'.

There is reason to believe that the ways in which people structure their environment are products of their culture. Greenfield, Reich and Olver (1966) and Maccoby and Modiano (1966), for instance, have obtained results which suggest that people in a peasant culture form less general concepts than people in an urban, technological culture. This monograph is restricted to a discussion of development in advanced, technological cultures. In addition to the differences in systems of exchange and production, cultures also vary, of course, in their social rules of conduct and in their values. The process of social interaction by which children conform to social rules and evaluate and adopt values is also not considered in this monograph. Discussion is restricted to the analysis and classification of behaviour that is directed towards objects and events in the environment.

Directed actions have consequences of two kinds: extracting more information, as in investigating a strange event, or producing a change in sense-organ stimulation. Both may be achieved without making any change in the environment, as in turning to look in a different direction. In other instances an environmental event is produced by an action; examples are sounds or movements of objects or a change in their spatial arrangement. Seeking information ranges from looking longer at something that is not immediately recognized to scientific inquiry; producing a variation in sensory input ranges from shaking a rattle to listening to a symphony and looking at a picture.

The questions of why people investigate and seek knowledge and why they seek variation in sensory input and develop aesthetic interests are important, but not essential for a discussion of the classification of behaviour patterns and how they develop. These questions will not be dealt with.

Sources of data

In order to classify behaviour along the lines that have been indicated, the necessary information must obviously be gathered when the behaviour of children is observed. What this is will be evident from the discussion of criteria. It will also be evident that only investigations in which these questions have been asked provide data for discussion and analysis. Those that make an inventory of items of behaviour at successive ages or establish norms of behaviour or standardize tests do not fall into this category.

No systematic observation is, of course, completely blind or undertaken without some framework, and some such framework guided the early selection of items for tests and inventories. The retention or exclusion of a test item depends, however, on statistical considerations. The study of the process of development, on the other hand, requires the experimental variation of the conditions under which a problem is presented. This requires a more precise formulation of the questions being asked by the investigator who consequently requires a conceptual framework within which to ask them.

Such formulation has been undertaken most extensively by Piaget since the early 1920s and later by Inhelder. Their concern is with the sequence of development and with the process of change. The questions they have asked and the methods they have devised to answer them have brought to light facts about human development that were not suspected. Their second contribution has been to define criteria for classifying behaviour and mediating processes. The main source of data for discussion in this monograph is thus the Genevan work and that stemming from it elsewhere. Such studies outside Geneva have tended to concentrate on the age groups of five to eight years. There have been few of younger children and none that investigate the details of the process in infancy. For this it is still necessary to draw on Piaget's very detailed day-to-day observations of his own three children. These observations in the home are regarded as uncontrolled by some; they certainly did not have the benefit of modern recording equipment. At the very least, however, they form an unrivalled source of hypotheses about development in infancy, few of which have been followed up.

This raises questions about the suitable size of samples. It is feasible to obtain a large sample of behaviour only for a *small* number of individuals; the larger the group of individuals, the smaller the amount of behaviour that can be sampled from each. Furthermore, the intervals between observations have to be fairly long when large groups are studied. A month is a long interval in infancy; developmental changes are so rapid that observations at such intervals will miss important steps in the process.

The need for frequent, almost daily, observation and the collection of large samples of behaviour from one child led to a renewed use of their own children as subjects by some investigators, for example, by Piaget (1953, 1955) and Valentine (1942) earlier and by Hutt (1967) more recently. The contemporary analytical study of the development of language also requires large samples of speech and it is similarly limited in the number of children who may be observed. In this area, too, investigators have used their own children as subjects (e.g. Lewis, 1963; Weir, 1962). There is obviously a need both for the study of small groups for details of the process to be elucidated and for the use of larger groups in order to examine hypotheses so obtained and to test the generality of the findings.

A further source of data that will be drawn upon is that gathered by the writer, using severely retarded children as subjects. Severe subnormality is a condition that frequently arises from some forms of cerebral pathology. It could be objected that such studies yield information only about subnormal children and that they do not help to elucidate the process of normal development. On the other hand, if the same sequences of development are found both in older subnormal children and in younger normal children, the difference being only in the rate of acquisition, it could be argued that cerebral pathology slows down the rate of development, but does not affect the course of events. If so, the study of slowly developing children may provide confirmatory evidence. The occurrence of certain developments together, both in older subnormal and in younger normal children, would support the view that the developments were related and not merely contemporaneous.

A further source that has influenced methods of observation and analysis in child psychology has been the study of sub-human species. Recent findings in this area are relevant to the study of the process of human development. Finally, the 'information-processing' approach adopted by Bruner, Goodnow and Austin (1956), in the study of adult thinking, has recently been extended to the investigation of children. However, despite the rapid growth of research interest in the process of development in recent years, some of the questions to be raised will be left unanswered through lack of data concerning them.

Summary and outline

It may be appropriate at this point to give a summary of what is being attempted in this monograph. Development is considered to result from a continuous process of interaction between physiological maturation and the organism's inter-actions with its environment. Consequently a dichotomy between 'unlearned' and 'learned' behaviour is not considered useful. Analyses will be made of successive forms of organized behaviour, namely, of actions that are directed towards external objects or other parts of the body. The analysis will be made in the light of the points made by Miller, Galanter and Pribram (1960) concerning the hierarchical structure of behaviour, and the concepts of the feedback loop in the TOTE will be used. When new forms have been distinguished from existing ones, questions concerning the process by which one develops into the other will be asked. The aim is to explain the approach rather than to give a detailed account of human development in the context of this framework and, hopefully, to stimulate others to ask and attempt to answer these kinds of questions.

The next two chapters will deal with behaviour that is 'sense-dominated' in Hebb's terminology. In them a detailed analysis is made of behaviour patterns of the first year. Some readers may wish to omit this section and begin with chapter 4, which will examine the process of change from these behaviour patterns to the early forms of 'mediated' behaviour; if so they will find a summary at the end of chapter 4. The fifth chapter discusses the further development of the mediational processes that precede others which Piaget terms 'operations'. The final one will consider the development of these and their further modification into higher-order adult forms.

Since several of Piaget's observations in *The Origins of Intelligence in the Child* and in *The Construction of Reality in the Child* are described in the next three chapters, these will be referred to by the appropriate initials (OI and CR) together with the number of the observation.

2 Looking and Listening

Neonatal behaviour and response to stimulation

The behavioural repertoire of the newborn infant is surprisingly large: a list made by Munn (1961) consists of seventy-five items. Many of these are reflex responses that contribute to the survival of the infant. Only those that play a part in the development of the direction of actions towards other parts of the body and towards external objects will be discussed. This excludes the avoidance reactions that protect the organism from damage. Reactions *away* from sources of intense or painful stimulation can play little part in the development of actions *towards* objects. This virtually leaves us with the grasp, sucking and head-turning responses; these, together with responses in the visual and auditory systems, are the main specific responses to external stimulation that are important in this context.

The term 'reflex response' is being used when a certain sequence of movements is evoked by a particular kind of stimulation. An object in the mouth elicits the response of sucking that object and when an object stimulates the palm of the hand it is reflexly grasped. In addition to making such reactions to specific stimulation, the neonate performs gross movements of head and limbs which, unlike the above responses, are not elicited by specific stimulation. In the course of such undirected movements, the palm of the child's hand may by chance touch an object, which may then elicit the grasp reflex. Thus, at first, objects get into the child's hand or his mouth by chance contact or when an adult puts them there. It is not for some months that the infant can direct his hand towards objects within his reach that he sees and so bring them nearer. This chapter is concerned with how these undirected movements become directed actions upon the environment and the self.

One issue raised by the question of how complex behaviour patterns develop from the neonatal repertoire concerns learning in the newborn. A second one is the relative importance of the conditioning of responses, such as sucking and grasping, to stimuli other than the natural one and of the conditioning of the undirected movements. After a lag of many years, research has again been undertaken into conditioning in the neonate. (See Brackbill and Fitzgerald, 1969, and Lipsitt, 1963, for reviews.) Whereas results of the earlier studies left in doubt the question of whether the newborn infant could learn, recent experiments have produced evidence that conditioned responses can be established in the first few days of life (Lipsitt, 1966; Siqueland and Lipsitt, 1966). Lipsitt attributed his positive results to the use of massed trials over the course of an hour instead of spaced trials over a period of days, as in the earlier studies.

The undirected movements referred to above correspond to Skinner's (1938) 'operants', which he distinguished from responses that are elicited by external stimuli. Siqueland and Lipsitt (1966) have, however, made the point, at least for the head-turning response, that it is difficult to distinguish between respondent and operant behaviour in neonates. Further, there is disagreement as to whether classical and operant conditioning involve different kinds of learning or are merely different experimental procedures for studying the same learning process. Nevertheless, in the study of the development of the human individual, a strong case may be made for upholding a distinction between the actions of the environment upon the child and the actions of the child upon his environment.

When existing reflex (respondent) responses are conditioned to other stimuli, the performance of the response does not influence the occurrence of the event, the unconditioned stimulus that follows it. The child's response cannot make the event happen; nor, in the case of aversive stimuli, can the response that is elicited by the conditioned stimulus prevent or delay the event. The conditioned sucking response, elicited by the sound of the mother's voice, does not produce the event of food in the mouth. The stimuli that are responded to merely signal the forthcoming event. The sight of a rattle also precedes the event of a sound if the rattle is shaken. But when the child has learned to perform the actions of grasping and shaking the rattle, he himself produces the event of the sound. This is the important difference. It is through the learning in connection with undirected movements that the child acts *upon* his environment and produces changes in it.

Moreover, when a response is made to a previously neutral stimulus that precedes one that already elicits the response, there is no major alteration in the response itself. The change is in the form of partial elicitation, as when the sucking but not the swallowing part of the sequence is evoked by a non-nutritive object, or of decrease in amplitude or total inhibition. In the development of organized behaviour it is the coordinated performance of previously separate movements that is important. When an object is grasped on visual contact, movements of different parts of the body, the head and the hand and arm, are coordinated; the free movement of hand and arm in space has become directed towards the object. Thus it is maintained that the undirected, free movements are the stuff out of which organized behaviour is made.

In view of this, it may be asked whether external stimulation has, in addition to its specific effect upon certain responses, any effect on this general activity in the first few days. If visual, auditory and tactile stimuli, below the pain and 'startle' levels of intensity, influence gross motor activity, increasing it or decreasing it, this may be a necessary condition for the development of specific movements directed towards the objects that are sources of the stimulation. Such an effect would at least indicate that the stimulus captures the 'attention' of the neonate. Although investigation of the orienting reaction to novel stimuli and of its relation to learning and states of arousal has been in progress for some time (Berlyne, 1960, 1963; Sokolov, 1963), study of attentive processes in the newborn infant is of more recent origin. Making qualitative observations of changes in gross motor activity, Wolff (1966) reported that neonates in an alert waking state showed a decrease in general activity in response to sounds, touch and when following a moving object. Other investigators have used recording equipment in order to obtain more exact measures of change. Haith (1966) found that an intermittent moving visual stimulus had an arresting effect upon non-nutritive sucking, and Semb and Lipsitt (1968) obtained evidence that a sound led both to the cessation of such sucking when it was in progress and to the onset of it when it was not. They attributed the difference between their results and previous negative findings with regard to the sucking response to the use of a different response measure.

Apart from this question of attentive processes in the newborn infant, his actions of looking and listening, together with reflex grasping and sucking, are all at first evoked when objects chance to come into his visual or auditory field, his hand or his mouth. The point is how the child moves from this to directing his head and hands towards objects, so that sensory input from them results from his own action and not from chance contact or adult initiation.

There are two questions which may be asked about such directed action. One concerns the degree of coordination involved in the action; the other is what action is performed upon the object. The first one is being treated in this chapter.

The important coordination which is discussed in this chapter is that of hand and eyes, of grasping objects that are looked at (occurring sometime during the fifth or sixth month). The complexity of this apparently simple behaviour pattern, which an adult performs many times every day, has already been pointed out. Analysis of it indicates what prior behaviour patterns need to be examined. It requires visual fixation of the object, activation of hand movements on visual contact with the object, bringing the hand near the object, with the result that both are in the same visual field, directing the hand at the object and performing the opening and closing movements of the hand in the grasping action. Thus we need to consider the earlier development of all these component activities. Our concern in the first place is thus with the direction of eyes, head, hands and arms towards objects.

Less obviously relevant, but equally important, is the development of motor control, particularly of the hand. Such control is necessary for directed movements towards objects and for 'holding' actions. There is control of movement when the hand is moved in a specific direction through space towards the mouth or a visually fixated object. The control in holding actions requires the prevention of movement. Continued visual fixation of a stationary object requires that the head is held still; similarly, continued retention of an object in the hand involves continued innervation of the necessary muscles. A point that will be reiterated is that a 'holding' action of this kind is just as positive an action as is movement.

Finally, developments from the sucking response and coordinations of sucking with other activities must be included. This may seem strange when the subject of discussion is hand–eye coordination. Piaget (1953) has argued, however, that grasping an object that is in the mouth is a necessary prior development to grasping the object that is looked at. Moreover, Piaget (1953) and Bruner (1968), among others, have pointed out that the mouth, as well as the hand and eyes, may be used for exploring objects. Bruner (1968) also discussed evidence which suggests that non-nutritive sucking may serve to relieve distress or distract 'attention' from a painful source of stimulation.

A further point about sucking should also be noted. It is far from being a simple response to stimulation. It is a complex sequence of movements, which includes swallowing when milk is sucked from the object. Although it is often not immediately evoked by the first stimulation of the mouth (Gunther, 1961), the performance of such a coordinated sequence shortly after birth suggests that the behaviour is already organized at birth (Bruner, 1968, Kessen, 1967, Piaget, 1953). Kessen (1967) has made the same point about looking. Thus the study of the development of organized behaviour through interactions with the environment, takes its departure from existing organized patterns of behaviour, which are the basic phylogenetic equipment of the species.

Furthermore, Bruner and Bruner (1968) have drawn attention to the important fact that not only are there established organized sequences of behaviour at birth, but also the co-ordinated performance of more than one. They point out, however, that the sequences that are coordinated are mainly regulated by the autonomic nervous system and that such coordination is essential for survival. The example they quote is the continuation of breathing while sucking, without one activity disrupting the other.

It is against this phylogenetic background that we examine the development of organized behaviour in the individual in the course of his interactions with the environment. We turn from it to look at the coordinations in the development of grasping objects that are looked at. The component activities and possible prior developments have been indicated. Head-turning responses, particularly in looking, will be discussed first; the second section will consider the control of hand movements and grasping upon tactile and oral contact; the final section will deal with the activation of hand movements upon visual contact with the object and with the final coordinations.

Looking at objects and hands

Head-turning is elicited by tactile stimulation of the cheek, by sounds and by stimulation of the peripheral visual receptors. The first may bring an object into central (foveal) vision.

The development of visual perception is a separate question – or perhaps it would have been considered so until recently. The role of learning in perceptual development (Gibson, 1969) and the hypothesis that feedback from eye movements may be involved (Held and Hein, 1963) bring the process in the organization of the visual world very close to that in the organization of behaviour. Moreover Piaget (1953, 1955) has argued that sensory coordination of input in different modalities from the same object results from the coordination of sucking with grasping, vision and grasping, and so forth.

The development of visual perception cannot, however, be treated in this monograph. Changes brought about by external stimulation upon the eye movements of the newborn infant do, however, require a brief reference. The technical equipment that makes it possible to record the eye movements of infants and so to obtain data on where the eye is directed has only recently been devised. With this advance, the study of early looking has become an active research area (e.g. Saltapek and Kessen, 1966). In the absence of patterned stimulation, such as a white or black expanse, the eye movements of the neonate are wide ranging; the effect of a simple stimulus, such as an outline triangle or circle divided by a vertical line, is to restrict the 'roving' movements, though the whole figure is not scanned; parts of it, particularly corners and contours, are looked at.

One subsequent development in looking is an extension to other parts of a single object. A second is from one object to another and following a moving object; these involve movements of the head as well as of the eyes and they thus enter into this discussion as behaviour patterns of looking. Study of the extension of looking to objects further away in a room or outside it has as yet received little attention; research interest has tended to focus on the influence of novelty and complexity (Berlyne, 1958; Fantz, 1963; Schaffer and Parry, 1969). Equally important, though also neglected, is the observation of the early visual following by the infant of sequences of events, particularly of the actions of people. This is important for the development of imitation and possibly also in learning to distinguish between events produced by the self and those produced by others.

More data are thus required before a classification may be made of the early looking behaviour patterns. Nevertheless, a tentative one may be discussed on the basis of the present evidence. The observations of White, Castle and Held (1964), for instance, suggest that a distinction may have to be made between the ways in which a moving object is kept in view. They found that visual pursuit of a moving object is, in the first instance, a matter of jerks; when the object has moved into peripheral vision, the infant then moves his head and so brings the object into foveal vision and keeps it still until the object is once more in peripheral vision, whereupon he moves his head again, and so on. Smooth following is a later development.

The jerky following would appear to be of the same order as turning the head in the direction of the peripheral visual receptors that are stimulated by a stationary object, the only difference being that the action is repeated several times in the conditions of a repetition of peripheral stimulation by the moving object. Keeping the moving object in central vision by moving at the appropriate speed would seem to require regulation of the speed of the movement and on this count it would seem to be of a higher order. It is comparable to moving a pointer at the correct speed to track a moving target, achieving a smooth performance after earlier jerky movements resulting in under-shooting and over-shooting. Whether the visual following of the infant involves minimal speeding up and slowing down as the object gets ahead or behind is a matter of conjecture, to be settled by further observation.

It may be, too, that successive looking at different stationary objects and glancing alternately between two take different forms with development.

When the infant begins to look successively from one object to another, does the next one come into peripheral vision while the current one is still in central vision? In the 'alternate glance', is the other object in peripheral vision when one is being fixated? If so, such activity on the basis of a peripheral cue would have to be classified differently from successive and alternate looking in the absence of such a cue. Piaget (1953) appears to be making such a distinction when he speaks of 'directed' looking in the second and third months, when the child looks successively at different objects and alternates between two. If the 'alternate glance' does not involve continued peripheral stimulation by the one not fixated, then the question of the critical time interval between glances is raised.

With regard to the visual following of the movements of people, Piaget (1953) reports an observation of his son at the age of nearly three months. The child watched him while he was eating his breakfast and followed the movements of his hand back and forth between his mouth and the plate. Further observations of looking of this kind are clearly necessary.

Even on present evidence, however, infants appear, then, to be doing a good deal of looking at objects before they grasp the object they look at. An important development in this latter behaviour is when their own hands become objects of visual interest; from this may develop the control of hand movements. Some time during his third month the child begins to hold his hand still and to look at it, briefly at first and then for longer periods. This is more complex behaviour than looking at external objects, since the hand has also to be held still in the visual field. 'Holding' actions of the head, in visual fixation, and of the hand illustrate a single feedback loop, involving kinaesthetic feedback from the muscles concerned. When the hand is held still and looked at, two such feedback loops are involved, that in fixating a visual object, the hand, and that in holding the hand still. Elucidation of the conditions under which the infant first looks briefly at his own hand require further day-to-day observation of more children. Piaget's observation suggests that sucking activities lead to it; the child catches sight of his hand as it comes from his mouth. The chance occurrence is no doubt true, but it could occur in the course of other movements.

In addition to holding his hand still in order to look at it, the infant also does things with his hand which he watches, for example, he twiddles his fingers and opens and closes his hand. These hand-looking activities have also been observed by the writer in older extremely backward children who are unable to grasp objects they see, as are normal infants when they first develop this. This kind of correspondence strongly suggests a relation between activities rather than the accidental occurrence of both in time. The child at this point in development also visually follows his moving hand, though he cannot keep his hand in view. Control of hand and arm movements in this activity appears to develop later than such control in other activities. It is possible that the first directed movements of hand and arm are made towards the mouth and then towards objects that have just touched the hand. Accordingly, these two directed actions will be examined next.

Grasping on tactile and oral contact

The behaviour of directing the hand to the mouth requires the coordination of both hand and arm movements. Either the head has to be held still or it has to be moved in the same direction as the moving hand. It is necessary that the arm is directed at least to the face and when the hand reaches the face it has to land in the mouth and not in the eye or nose. Further study is required of how hit-and-miss attempts change into a single smooth movement to the mouth. The process by which the child comes to do this is not clear. Piaget's observations suggest that this learning, in the second month, tends to occur in states of hunger when the child's mouth is open and his hand waving about. This situation would at least increase the opportunity for chance contacts. Whether the child learns a route through space by means of such cues as chin, clothes, bedclothes, etc., as Piaget (1953) suggests, is a matter of conjecture; if so it is something akin to learning a maze! The outcome of this coordination is that the child now, in respect to one of his reflex responses, is able to produce himself the stimulus that evokes the response, so that he is no longer dependent upon chance contact with the object.

Although the child in his second month retains the object that is placed in his palm (B. L. White, 1969), grasping is for some time still dependent upon chance tactile contact with the object. However, grasping when the object has just touched the fingers or back of the hand is an advance over reflex grasping of an object in the palm. The process by which one develops from the other has also still to be elucidated. For some suggestions as to what might occur, we must turn to Piaget. He reports that repeated manual contact with the object in the second month seemed to produce increased activity of the hand. At times the movements seemed to be in the direction of the object, although they did not land on it (Ob. 50, OI)[1].

1 See page 42.

Further study of the excitatory effect of manual contact with the object at this stage is clearly needed, as it is one of the conditions that lead to the repetitive opening and closing of the fist, which is reported to occur at this time. This behaviour is clearly important: non-reflex grasping cannot occur if the hand remains fisted!

Behaviour which may be important in the transition from reflex to voluntary grasping is that reported in another observation of Piaget (Ob. 52, OI): when an object had been reflexly grasped and was about to fall from his hand, the infant grasped it again. If confirmed, this behaviour might be an essential step in the movement of the hand in space towards an object that has just touched the back or side of the hand.

Piaget further reports that a new behaviour pattern precedes voluntary grasping. This is to scratch at something, such as a sheet, to try to grasp, let go, scratch, try to grasp, and so on, until the activity peters out. With time (two to three weeks) the scratching drops out and the child goes straight from tactile contact of the hand with the object (not on the palm) to grasping it and holding it (Ob. 53 and 54, OI).

Trivial as it may seem to an adult, this, the first 'voluntary' non-reflex grasping is an important development. As can be seen, even the details of the behaviour that precedes it have not been examined for more than a few children, so that an outline of the learning process is speculative. If there is confirmation of another of Piaget's observations, that contact of the object with the palm of the hand in the first few weeks has an arresting effect on other activity in progress, this would be important: it means that the 'event' is 'attended' to. Equally important, if confirmed, is the observation that, subsequently, tactile contact leads to increased activity of the hand. This last activity may not be essential, except that it increases the possibility of chance contact with an object that has just been handled. When an object is grasped reflexly on contact with the palm, the insides of the fingers are also stimulated by the object. Thus the action of grasping, with its attendant kinaesthetic feedback, is succeeded by this tactile stimulation. When the object is held, there must be both tactile stimulation from the object and kinaesthetic feedback from the 'holding' action. A feedback loop from one to the other may be postulated.

It is conceivable that non-reflex grasping may develop from the conditioning of the grasp reflex to the event of the object touching the fingers. A grasping action when the object begins to fall from the hand may develop from this and the subsequent contact of an object on the fingers may evoke this closing action of the hand. (It may be noted in passing that grasping is still of a palmar variety at this time, not involving the thumb. It is still so when objects are grasped on visual contact. The beginning of thumb and forefinger grasp does not appear until about thirty-six weeks and this grasping is not precise until twelve months – Halverson, 1931.)

Once objects are grasped on chance tactile contact with the hand, objects can get into the mouth by this route instead of on chance contact with the lips. Such oral contact with objects, however, may still be a matter of chance, depending on whether the hand reaches the mouth before the object. Piaget reports that sometimes the hand is sucked first and sometimes the object, depending upon the position of the hand and object (Ob. 63, OI).

Objects that the child is likely to touch with his hand in his first few months are his face, his other hand and an adult's hand. Piaget (Ob. 55 to 59, OI) reports these activities, together with mutual hand grasp. He also reports an interesting series of observations on the child appearing to react to the sight of the hand of another person as if it were his own. After repeated presentations, visual and tactile, of his father's hand over a period of several days, one child grasped it (Ob. 74, OI). Such behaviour presents problems of interpretation. It would be a mistake, as Piaget points out, to infer from this that the child had coordinated vision and grasping: other objects were looked at but not grasped. In Piaget's view, the sight of the hand of someone else evoked in the child the behaviour pattern of grasping one of his own hands with the other. Another child reacted to the sight of her father's hand by sucking her own (Ob. 76, OI).

The strong visual interest of the child of two to four months in his own hands was mentioned earlier. The developments in grasping that have just been discussed (e.g. scratching at objects) are additional manual activities that the child may incidentally see. It is possible, too, that the child may see an object in his hand and from this learn to react with hand movements to the sight of an object.

Piaget maintains that two other developments precede grasping on sight. One is that the child is able to keep his moving hand in view, in order to continue looking at it. The other is grasping objects on oral contact with them. Although there are few data on the sequence of these events in the development of infants, analysis and comparison of the various behaviour patterns support Piaget's point. These two behaviour patterns may be seen, upon analysis, to be less complex than grasping on sight and more complex than any discussed so far.

Contrast the behaviour of visually following the moving hand while not keeping it in view and while keeping it in view. In both cases the child has to move his head and eyes at the appropriate speed in order to keep the moving object in view. When he keeps his moving *hand* in view, he has also to move it at the correct speed to keep it in the visual field. Thus two feedback loops are involved, while following and holding actions require only one (visual fixation and following, retaining an object in the hand, etc.).

When grasping an object on oral contact, the child has to move his hand a greater distance than he does to grasp one that is touching his hand. He could not do this unless he could direct his hand to his mouth. Having done this, he then has to perform the grasping action. Two previous behaviour patterns are thus necessarily involved and grasping an object that is in the mouth may accordingly be regarded as more complex than either of its component parts.

Few studies appear to have been made to test the generality of Piaget's sequence from grasping on tactile contact, to oral contact and finally to visual contact with the object. The writer has some data on ten subnormal children, aged seven months to three-and-a-half years, who did not grasp objects on visual contact. Six grasped objects that touched the side of their hands, though only one grasped an object on oral contact. Observations were made of this last child (a mongol) from the age of seven months to three years four months. At the age of seven months she grasped only on tactile contact; grasping on oral contact occurred a month later. At nine months she did not grasp objects she saw, though this was recorded when she was eleven months old.

This same sequence was evoked in two other children in the course of half an hour. One of these was aged fifteen years, and when first observed did not grasp visually presented objects. An object was then taken towards the child's hand, where she visually followed it; since she did not grasp it, it was placed in her mouth. She did not then take it so her hand was touched with it, whereupon she did grasp it. Subsequently in the course of half an hour she grasped an object placed in her mouth, then one placed near her hand when she could see both together and finally, she grasped an object which she saw when her hand was not in the same field of vision as the object.

The same procedure was followed with another child aged three-and-a-half years, who at first appeared unable to grasp objects on sight, and the same grasping sequence was elicited.

In order to find out whether or not an infant can grasp objects on oral contact, the investigator places part of a suitable object in the child's mouth; in the everyday situation the child presumably puts one there himself. According to Piaget, these are reciprocal developments: the child who can grasp an object that is in his mouth can also convey to it an object that he has grasped on chance tactile contact. He quotes observations to the effect that a change occurs in the way the child holds the object when he is taking it to his mouth. From this point, he holds it so that it enters the mouth first; before, it was a matter of chance whether his hand or the object reached his mouth first and sometimes he licked both together (Ob. 63 to 66, OI). Thus, Piaget's interpretation is that earlier the child was merely directing his hand towards his mouth and the presence of the object was incidental; subsequently he directs the *object* towards his mouth. B. L. White (1969), who reported a study of about twenty infants aged one-and-a-half to four-and-a-half months, did not make this distinction: bringing the object to the mouth is reported when the children were first observed between one and two months. Grasping on oral contact was not investigated.

A series of studies on the coordination of sucking and looking has been reported by Bruner (1968) and it would be of interest to know whether this coordination is achieved around the same time as that between sucking and grasping. In the Harvard studies reported by Bruner an ingenious piece of equipment was devised so that at the sucking end of it the situation for the infant was no different from that in the ordinary feeding situation. The baby was on the mother's lap, and she held the bottle to his mouth. Inside it were arrangements for delivering milk in pre-arranged ways, and tubes and wires for the delivery of milk and recording of responses came out of the other end, connected up with the rest of the equipment. Both suctioning pressure and mouthing (termed negative and positive sucking respectively) were separately recorded. It was observed that the infant kept his eyes closed while sucking for the first few days after birth. Within a few weeks the eyes were open, but visual fixation or following tended to interrupt sucking. Thus there was suppression of one activity by another, mainly of sucking by looking. A second phase, occurring usually sometime in the third month, was an alternation between the two activities. The third phase was a coordination of the looking with sucking, by means of behaviour which Bruner terms 'place-holding'. In this only negative sucking (suctioning) was suppressed by looking; mouthing continued, with a little decrease in amplitude, while the infant looked. The interpretation of this behaviour in terms of place-holding is important and it will be discussed further in chapter 3. By it is meant that the infant continues one part of an activity in progress, while he performs another different one, and that the continuation serves as a reminder to resume the f activity. Such a finding indicates caution about interpreting the resumption of interrupted activities in infants in terms of memory in the absence of cues in the current situation.

A further instance of the coordination of sucking with looking is provided by the results of another experiment reported by Bruner. The apparatus was so arranged that the infants could bring an out-of-focus picture into focus by sucking a few times on a dummy, which they learned to do. In another condition sucking made the picture blurred and refraining from sucking made it clear again. In the younger infants looking again first suppressed sucking, with the consequence that the picture became blurred. Subsequently the infants could perform the coordinated activities of looking and sucking for increasingly long periods of time. This seems to be an instance of self-regulatory behaviour. The child, in Bruner's words, 'seems to be learning not so much a *specific* response but rather a sequentially organized, adaptive strategy of responses' (1968, p. 24).

Grasping on sight

Of the main developments that must precede grasping on sight, three have been dealt with. These are visual fixation of an object, opening and closing the hand and the control of hand movements. Such control is not necessarily a matter of looking at the hand while moving it. When an object is grasped on visual contact without having touched the hand or mouth, it is the object that is looked at, not the hand. To speak of visually directed grasping is thus misleading. It is not that the hand is visually directed on its way to the object, but that it is brought to the place occupied by the object that is looked at. Adults do not look for their hands when they grasp objects they see and no one has reported observations that infants do so. Control of hand movements has been evidenced already in the first few months when the infant directs his hand towards his mouth and keeps his moving hand in his visual field. The further control with which we are now concerned is that in bringing it from outside the visual field to grasp the object that is seen.

It might be supposed that the essential first step towards this development is activation of the hands upon visual contact with an object. How this develops is also not clear and we have little information on it. Piaget (1953) reports that visual contact with an object evokes sucking movements before it elicits hand movements; a test of the generality of this finding does not appear to have been made. It may be that the essential link between the visual object and hand is established through the child's visual interest in his hands. This may have led him by chance to look at his hand when it is holding an object that has been grasped on chance tactile contact. B. L. White (1969) reported that 13 per cent of his group at the age of one-and-a-half to two months looked at an object in the hand and the percentage is between 70 and 80 from the age of two-and-a-half months onwards. Whether the child sees the object and hand as differentiated is another point. It is possible, in the second and third months, at any rate, that the sight of the hand evokes the behaviour pattern of holding the hand still and looking at it; it cannot be assumed that the presence of the object, placed in the infant's hand by an adult, evokes the looking. Intensive longitudinal observation in the natural setting and experimental intervention would seem necessary to decide between these alternative interpretations. Alternate looking at and sucking an object that is held is reported by both Piaget and White in the fourth month, by which time Bruner (1968) found that these two activities in a different situation, could be coordinated.

Shortly after this behaviour Piaget reports that the sight of an object produces a manual response, some fluttering of the hands. He also observed that sucking movements were even more pronounced. These are very marked, too, in subnormal children at this period. The child's eyes seem to bulge as he looks at the object fixedly and his mouth protrudes; it is very difficult to avoid the inference that the child has a strong desire to suck the object.

Having shown an object to a child and observed the sucking response and fluttering of hands, Piaget moved the object nearer to her hand, where she followed it visually. She then alternately looked at her hand and the object (a rattle). Hand and object were thus seen together in the same visual field. Even with this degree of proximity, however, she did not move her hands towards the object and grasp it, though her fingers twitched. When her hand touched the rattle, she grasped it at once (Ob. 69, O I). Piaget's subsequent observations were that the child's hand became increasingly activated on visual contact with an object if preceded by tactile contact with it. For example, Piaget showed a child an object which she did not grasp. Without her seeing his movement, he placed it in her outstretched hand, removed it and put it into her visual field again. Her hands moved as a result of the contact (Ob. 77, O I).

The conditions in which the object is grasped and the kind of motor response evoked by the sight of an object are of such theoretical importance that further study is clearly required.

Piaget has drawn attention to another developmental sequence in grasping: that the child first grasps the object he looks at when both his hand and the object happen to be in the same visual field; grasping a seen object when the hand is outside the visual field occurs later. This sequence has been confirmed by White, Castle and Held (1964) and the writer has also observed the sequence in severely subnormal children. After this Piaget reports that the sight of an object activates the child's hands in a more pronounced manner and that the child behaves as if he is searching with his hands for the object; when he sees them together, he grasps the object, but when he has done so sucking activities with it predominate.

Bruner (1968) reported that little alternate looking at hand and object was observed in the Harvard studies of grasping and he attributed the discrepant findings to the fact that the infants in the studies he reports were supported in a semi-upright position, while those observed by Piaget and by White, Castle and Held were lying on their backs. There are, however, two behaviour patterns to be distinguished. One is the alternate looking at hand and object. The other is grasping the object when it is placed beside the child's hand, after having been presented for visual fixation, when the hand was not near it. Further observations are required on both.

The other explanation of the finding by some investigators of a behaviour pattern that is not observed by others may be that some behaviour patterns occur for a brief period and this period may be between observations. This is more likely to be the case with behaviour patterns that are superseded than with those that remain in the repertoire. Piaget (1953), for instance, reports a behaviour pattern in one child that lasted for only three days. After he had begun to grasp an object that was placed near his hand, the child brought his hand towards the object from another position, but before he grasped it he placed it *beside* the object. If grasping on visual contact with the object occurs first when the hand and object are seen together, the child in this case himself brought about the situation in which he was able to grasp objects he looked at: when he could see both at once. This behaviour pattern was subsequently omitted and the child placed his hand straightway on the object.

Grasping the object that is looked at, by bringing the hand (or hands) from any position in space to that of the object, is the end-point of the sequence of behaviour patterns examined in this chapter. Piaget (1953) has suggested that two other reciprocal developments accompany this acquisition. He experimentally held the child's outstretched hand, preventing movement, before and after the child grasped seen objects. After this event the children looked in the direction of the hand that was held, while before it they struggled to free the hand without looking at it. His second suggestion is that, when the child grasps on sight, he brings the object nearer and looks at it, instead of putting it in his mouth as previously. B. L. White (1969), however, observed extensive looking in a larger group of children before this. 'Viewing' the object in hand, in his investigation, is described as glancing at the object 'one or more times' or regarding it 'steadily for up to two minutes'. Brief glancing is clearly a different matter from steady regard; the point about what is regarded in early looking was made earlier. Further study is clearly required to establish when the infant looks at the object in his hand and the duration of his fixation.

Classification of behaviour patterns

Despite the frequent comment in this chapter concerning the need for further research, it is unlikely that even a tentative outline of the sequence of other developments may be attempted, as it may for grasping on sight. It is perhaps incautious to do this on the basis of the present evidence. Nevertheless, a summary will perhaps serve to remind the reader of the behaviour patterns that have been described, before we proceed to discuss the classification of them. Over a period of four or five months the infant has moved from the separate activities of looking at, grasping and sucking objects, to grasping objects that he sees. Pronounced visual interest in objects is present early and this is extended to his own hands, again pronounced. The infant not only watches his stationary hand, but watches it while he does things with it, such as moving it, or the fingers, or opening it and closing it or scratching at objects. A beginning of control over the direction of arm and hand movements is established when the infant puts his hand to his mouth. Once he can do this and grasp objects that touch his hands, sucking and looking can extend to objects so grasped. Further research is required to establish whether or not grasping the object in the mouth is an essential step in the process of grasping on sight. When the infant can keep his moving hand in view, he has further control over hand movements. The previously acquired behaviour pattern of holding the hand still in order to look at it is used when the object is alternately sucked and looked at. An essential development is responding with hand movements to the sight of an object, though how this occurs has still to be elucidated. Once vigorous hand movements are so evoked, it would seem but a short step to chance to see hand and object together, and then to grasp the object and to bring the hand from outside the visual field towards the object that is looked at without the intervening behaviour pattern.

Different conditions of rearing and of variation in stimulating objects in the child's environment produce variation in the age at which these developments occur (B. L. White, 1969): such differences may also produce variation in the order in which some behaviour patterns are acquired, except when some are dependent upon the prior occurrence of others. Chance events may be a further factor in variation. Many of the developments that have been discussed appear to be the result of chance occurrences, in that they result from activities in progress. Yet the activities are such that the chance event must inevitably occur at some point in time.

Although research findings will finally settle the question of the order in which the various behaviour patterns are acquired, some, logically, must occur before others. Some instances of this have been pointed out when behaviour patterns have been analysed into their constituent components. From such analysis, predictions may be made concerning the sequence of development. A summary of this analysis is given in Table 1. A tentative classification has been made into five levels. The criteria being used for classification have been indicated earlier in the chapter. One is whether a behaviour pattern consists of simpler ones. A second is the number of feedback loops involved. Further analysis and investigation may reveal others, such as whether a cue is necessary in, for example, successive and alternate looking.

Those in the first level are of single directed actions towards an object on input from it, or of repetitions of an action that can be depicted in the form of a simple feedback loop between events and the action. Single directed actions are turning the head upon tactile stimulation by an object on the cheek, upon auditory stimulation and upon peripheral visual stimulation. The group of repetitive actions include those in which the child's action produces sensory input from his own body, for example, opening and closing his fist and similar actions with his hands; repetitive vocalizing is another example. It is assumed that auditory, tactile or visual feedback is the cue for the repetition of the action.

A second group includes 'holding' actions: visual fixation – which requires keeping the head still – retention of an object in the hand or mouth and that of holding the hand to the mouth. All but the last involve external objects. A single feedback loop is similarly postulated between input from the object

Table 1   Classification of Early Directed Behaviour

Single actions

I 1. Turning head in direction of cheek stimulated by object in line with mouth.
   2. Turning head and eyes towards sound.
   3. Turning head and eyes towards object that stimulates peripheral visual receptors.

II 1. Directing hand to mouth (learning from I1).
    2. Grasping object on *tactile* contact (from I10 and I5).

III 1. Grasping object on *oral* contact (I9 → II → II2).
     2. Taking to mouth object that is grasped on chance tactile contact. (II2 → I7 → II1).

IV 1. Grasping object in same visual field as hand (simultaneously I6 and III3 → II2).

V 1. Grasping object on visual contact (I6 simultaneously with learned actions that → IV1)

Repetitive actions

I 4. Repetition of vocalizations.
   5. Opening and closing fist (etc.).
   6. Holding: visual object (head still).
   7. Holding: hand in mouth.
   8. Holding: object in hand.
   9. Holding: object in mouth.
  10. Hand activated after tactile contact.
  11. Jerky visual following.
  12. Successive looking (on peripheral cue).
  13. Alternate glance (on peripheral cue).

II 3. Smooth visual following of object or hand (hand *not* kept in view) from I10? and 11).
    4. Looking at hand and keeping it still (simultaneous coordination of I6 and another type I 'holding' action – of hand).

III 3. Keeping moving hand in view while visually following it (II3 and II4 simultaneously).
     4. Holding object and looking at it (I6 and II4 simultaneously).
     5. Reacting with sucking movements on visual contact with object.
     6. Reacting with hand movement on visual contact with object.

and the muscles involved in holding. Scratching at an object that makes tactile contact with the fingers seems to be a similar pattern. Jerky visual pursuit of a moving object has also been classified among the repetitive behaviour patterns of level I, since it is the repetition of the action of turning to look at a stationary object upon a cue in peripheral vision; such following is achieved by moving in the same direction to bring the object into central vision. With successive looking the object is different each time, but if this occurs on a peripheral cue the behaviour pattern has the same character, as does looking alternately at two objects.

Behaviour patterns have been placed in the second category if they entail the simultaneous coordination of movements or holding actions of two parts of the body, or a succession of two behaviour patterns of level I or regulatory action that involves movement of *one* part of the body in *two* directions. The coordination of movement or holding actions of two parts of the body occurs when the hand is directed towards the mouth and when both head and hand are kept still, in the behaviour pattern of looking at the stationary hand. Grasping an object on tactile contact comprises two level I behaviour patterns: scratching at the object on tactile contact and opening and closing the hand. Regulatory action, with movement of one part of the body in two directions, is presumably involved in smooth visual pursuit, if this entails minimal speeding up and slowing down on feedback of the object moving one way or the other away from central vision.

Those behaviour patterns placed in the third category are a succession of two of the level II behaviour patterns or the performance of a level II pattern simultaneously with another one. Grasping an object that is in the mouth requires first continuing to retain an object in the mouth (level I action), directing the hand towards the mouth (level II) and grasping the object on tactile contact (level II). Taking an object to the mouth is a succession of these behaviour patterns in a different order. Visual pursuit of the moving hand is a level II pattern, carried out while the action of keeping the moving hand in view is performed. This requires the reciprocal regulation of movements of head and hands – two feedback loops. Holding an object and looking at it involves three level I holding actions (of the hand around object, of head held still and hand held still within the visual field, the last two of which form a level II pattern). This is perhaps the most dubious inclusion in category three, and a case could perhaps be made for placing it at level II.

The only instance in the fourth category requires the simultaneous performance of a level I and a level III pattern (looking at objects while moving the hand towards the object) followed by grasping (level II). Grasping a seen object when the hand is not in the same visual field as the object has been placed in a separate fifth category on the grounds that there is an additional interpolated action of bringing the hand into the visual field of the object that is looked at.

Once grasping of visual contact has been developed, the way is open for visually guided manipulative and searching behaviours. These are the subject of the next two chapters.

3 Acting for Effect

The behaviour patterns discussed in the last chapter have the outcome of maintaining contact with external objects by looking, listening, sucking or holding, or with producing events from other parts of the body, such as moving the hand and looking at it. We have not yet discussed actions that are performed upon *objects*, such that they produce sounds and movements that may be heard and seen. The presentation of objects of one sort or another to infants of five months or so onwards elicits a variety of repetitive behaviour patterns, such as shaking those that rattle, banging or rubbing others on a surface, patting those that hang and making them swing.

The two aspects of these behaviour patterns are reacting with a given kind of action to certain kinds of stimulus situations and looking at or listening to the subsequent sight or sound. The concept of the feedback loop, or 'circular reaction' in Piaget's usage, applied to these manipulative behaviour patterns, is that the visual or auditory feedback is the condition for the repetition of the action.

Piaget (1953) describes as primary circular reactions the behaviour patterns that produce events from other parts of the body, distinguishing these from actions upon objects. Among the latter he has made a further useful distinction between behaviour patterns in which the same kind of action is repeated, with the outcome of the same kind of event, as when an object is banged on the same surface, and those in which both the action and the outcome vary, as when an object is banged on different surfaces. The former, which he terms secondary circular reactions, are the subject of this chapter. The first section will deal with the learning of such repetitive behaviour patterns; the second will discuss the development of more complex behavioural sequences when an obstacle prevents the performance of an action and when the usual outcome of an action does not occur. One important feature that will be stressed, as that which differentiates the later from the earlier behaviour, is the coordination of two behaviour patterns. A second is withholding the performance of an action, either delaying it until a different action has been performed or delaying the repetition of an action until an event that follows the first one has been observed more closely.

Simple repetition

The infant may act upon objects in his environment directly or indirectly. He acts directly when he shakes a rattle that he holds in his hand. The action is indirect when he shakes himself while lying in his pram, with the result that objects hanging from the hood move, or when crying, smiling, etc. produce events from people. The events produced by people may be their own sounds and movements of their bodies or they may be events that they produce from objects.

After the child has learned to perform again the action that was previously followed by a certain kind of outcome, he is likely at some time to be faced with the non-occurrence of the usual event. The reason for the non-occurrence is, however, different with regard to objects and people. In the case of objects, continued repetition of the same or different actions will not produce the event: continued patting at a rigid object will not make it swing. On the other hand, an adult who has stopped playing with an infant may start again in response to some action of the child or he may not. In the course of social interaction, the child may have acquired a repertoire of behaviours which act as signals to which the adult responds in his ministering activities; the adult may also respond if the child uses these in other situations. These learned behaviour patterns thus have more the character of the communication of a request.

Although the *situation* regarding the recurrence of events is different for people and objects, there is no reason to suppose that the learning is different; we cannot assume that the infant is 'making a request'. This raises the question of what the infant learns when he performs an action that, on previous occasions, produced an event from an object or person. Has he learned only the temporal connection between action and subsequent event or has he learned the difference between events produced by his actions upon objects and events produced by other people? It is probable that he has not learned this difference in the first seven to eight months of life. This section deals with learning in this period.

The learned behaviour patterns to be considered first are those actions that produce events from objects, either directly or indirectly. The period before objects are grasped on sight will be discussed separately from that when objects are so grasped. After this the child's behaviour upon the occurrence of events that are not produced by his actions will be dealt with. Questions to be raised will include the differentiation of the precise movement from a global action, the generalization to similar objects and the learning of an association between particular sounds and particular objects.

Indirect actions upon objects

Do children learn to act upon objects during their early months when they are acquiring the behaviour patterns discussed in the last chapter? The child can, of course, incidentally produce events from objects, in the course of movements in progress. The young infant frequently shakes himself and waves his arms about and, if a rattle happens to be in his hand or hanging from the hood of the pram in which he is lying, sounds will accompany the movements. We are not, of course, interested in sequences of this sort. Our concern is when visual or auditory feedback from the event that is incidentally produced by such movements becomes a condition for the repetition of the same kind of movement – when, in fact, it becomes a directed action through learning. Further, it is necessary to establish that when the infant shakes himself, this is a learned response and not just something that might loosely be described as an expression of pleasure.

Infants react with such movements when they see toys move or hear sounds and when an adult plays with them.

The operant conditioning techniques developed by Skinner (1938, 1953) and his associates were devised to overcome problems in the study of learning in lower animals. They have been applied to young infants, notably by Lipsitt (1963), but not with the aim of investigating the development of more complex behaviour patterns from simpler ones. One of Lipsitt's studies was of the behaviour of shaking a string, which produced a sound; this is similar to the behaviour patterns now being discussed. The observations were, however, made of children who were ten months old, by which time more highly organized patterns of behaviour have been acquired. The question at that period is how two of these lower-level behaviour patterns become coordinated and performed in a certain order.

Lipsitt (1963) has, however, drawn attention to the methodological problems in the study of operant conditioning in very young infants. In one study he used the response of kicking and an event of a mild electric shock, but the attempt was fruitless. Even if successful it would be of little help for the present analysis, since the study of avoidance learning is less useful for it than that of approach behaviour.

Grasping on sight clearly opens up possibilities for the production of events from objects but, on the face of it, such learned actions are not necessarily dependent upon being able to grasp objects that are seen. There would appear to be nothing to prevent the child from learning to shake a rattle that he has grasped on tactile or oral contact, or to repeat the action of shaking his whole body, which moves toys that hang from the hood of a cot or pram. Children repeat their own vocalizations before they grasp objects they see and Rheingold, Gewirtz and Ross (1959) have demonstrated that such vocalization increases if an adult makes a sound after each one. This behaviour may be interpreted as a simple feedback loop in which an external event of the same kind as shaking in a pram and making rattles swing and sound is involved. It might thus be expected that learning to repeat global bodily movements that reproduce events would occur before grasping on sight is developed.

For observations on this period we must turn to Piaget (1953). These support the above assumption. He reports observations on his children before and after they could grasp objects they saw. One of his criteria for the formation of the secondary circular reaction was that subsequent visual presentation of the object evoked the action of shaking the body before the event of swinging or rattling occurred; it was, therefore, not then a reaction to the movement or sound. Another was the performance of the action by the child if the sound or movement stopped after having occurred. These criteria were met in the children before they grasped on sight. For example (Ob. 94, OI), one of his daughters was in her fourth month and unable to grasp objects she saw – or even to keep her moving hand in view – when he hung some dolls from the hood of the cot in which she was lying. She reacted by moving her whole body, including her legs. This was interpreted as an 'expression of joy', though it incidentally swung the toys at which she looked. Fourteen days later he considered that evidence for learning existed.

When young infants learn to make these gross bodily movements that shake the pram they are in and so produce sounds from objects hanging from the hood, do they learn to differentiate the essential movement from the total movement of the whole body? Piaget reports such differentiation (Ob. 97, OI). According to his observations, however, children at this period, before they grasp on sight, do not learn behaviour patterns in relation to objects in their hands, nor apparently associate sounds with objects they chance to hold. His son had learned the behaviour pattern of shaking himself all over in response to the sound from a rattle hanging from his cot. At the period when he grasped objects that were in the same visual field as his hand, he grasped a rattle in this situation. He took the rattle to his mouth, but the sound incidentally produced by this movement aroused the behaviour pattern learned in relation to the hanging rattle: he shook himself all over, including his arms, though eventually he moved his arm 'astonished and slightly worried by the increasing noise' (Ob. 102, OI). Another of Piaget's children shook her whole body, including her feet, when the rattle in her hand made a noise. She had a 'demented expression of mingled fear and pleasure, but she continued' (Ob. 102, OI). On a previous occasion a rattle was placed in the hand of the first child. He chanced to shake it, laughed and apparently heard the sound, but he did not look at the rattle in his hand. He looked instead at the hood of the cot where such sounds usually came from. Similar behaviour was observed in another child who could not keep her hand in view. As her hand came and went between her face and the pillow, she shook herself as she did when the dolls swung. Piaget interpreted the shaking as a joyful reaction. But then she immediately looked at the dolls and at the hood (Ob. 91, OI).

If this finding is confirmed in a situation in which the possibility of an auditory cue is definitely excluded, it would indicate that the child learns the customary place where events occur. Secondly, it would imply that the incidental performance of a learned action evokes the action of looking for the place where the event usually occurs – in conventional terms, not only does s evoke r, but the performance of r upon a different instigation evokes the action of looking for the stimulus object!

The failure of these children to locate the sound of the rattle when it was in their hands and the behaviour of looking at the place where such sounds usually came from raise doubts about whether the child is learning to associate particular sounds with particular objects when these are apart from the spatial context in which they were learned. It may be that the young infant, initially at least, learns to react with some movement, such as shaking himself, to a global stimulus situation in a particular place. Only further investigation can determine whether they do this and, if so, whether they can learn to differentiate the particular objects concerned, dolls that swing, rattles that sound, from the context of the hood, top of cot, etc. – and whether the position of the event in relation to themselves is a relevant factor. If so, the action of head-turning might be implicated.

Piaget (1953) suggests, however, that the infant of three months has learned to do more than associate events with a particular spatial context – that he also has learned that particular sounds go with particular kinds of objects. He claims that when the infant of three months turns his head in the direction of a sound, he is doing more than localize the sound: he is looking for the object that makes the sound. He reports observations (47 and 48 in OI) to the effect that this coordination occurs first if the object has just been seen and then only if the object is moving when it is found. He used himself as the object, moving out of the child's visual field and then calling. If he stayed still, the child 'searches anywhere at all, manifesting much attention to my voice; then he perceives me while I am immobile and continues searching . . . after this I shake my head and thereafter he turns towards me whenever I call and seems satisfied as soon as he has discovered me'. Subsequently the movement was not necessary. 'He looked to his left, then to his right, then ahead, then below him; then he catches sight of my hair and lowers his eyes until he sees my motionless face. Finally he smiles.'

That the child of three months looks for the object whose sound he hears is a most interesting suggestion that merits further study with modern equipment – asking, for example, whether such learning occurs, in very young infants, only with respect to the human voice and human face. Unless the finding is confirmed it is pointless to speculate on the learning process: whether two sensory events are associated or whether each is first connected with an action.

Manipulative behaviour patterns

If the child learns to respond only to a stimulus complex in a particular place, rather than to the object as such, it would explain why manual behaviour patterns with objects in the hand are developed later than those of global bodily movements that lead to events. Piaget reports the occurrence of manipulative behaviour patterns after the development of grasping on sight; the writer, with a large group of subnormal children, found that such behaviour patterns as shaking a rattle, banging an object on a surface and swinging an object were not present, in any instance, in children who could not grasp objects that they looked at (Woodward, 1959). The acquisition of such behaviour patterns is, however, not necessarily dependent upon the ability to grasp on sight; both may be the outcome of developments in perception, such as greater articulation of separate objects in a spatial field.

Piaget (1953) classifies as 'secondary circular reactions' both the global bodily actions and the manipulative behaviour patterns, along with grasping on sight. The basis of his distinction between secondary and primary circular reactions (the behaviour patterns described in the last chapter) is whether events are produced from external objects or other parts of the body.

It would appear, however, that the behaviour patterns that are present before and after grasping on sight is developed can be distinguished on the basis of differences in complexity. Behaviour patterns in which the action upon the object is indirect (e.g. through moving a pram) require only that the movement of shaking is repeated upon visual or auditory feedback of the result. With manipulative behaviour patterns the object must be held while the action is performed, as when an object is banged on a surface, or the hand must be directed towards a hanging object, as when one is swung. If the child looks at the object that he swings, bangs or shakes, the behaviour is on a par with grasping an object that is seen. Such looking requires the prior development of keeping the moving hand in view (classified at level III in Table 1). Shaking or swinging an object that is held, while looking at the movement, thus involves the simultaneous performance of a level III pattern, a level I holding action and the action of swinging, banging, etc. This is a greater number of coordinated lower level actions than any up to level V (grasping on sight) in Table 1. It would thus be expected that the acquisition of these behaviour patterns would be related to grasping on sight.

The behaviour of shaking a string that is attached to a toy, with the result that the toy swings, appears on the face of it to be a more complex behaviour pattern than those discussed above, since it seems to involve the use of one object for moving another. But although the adult regards the string and toy as two separate objects, this is no guarantee that the child of five to seven months does so. Indeed, the behaviour of children of eight to ten months who perform two coordinated sequences of the kinds of behaviour pattern now under discussion suggests that they treat two objects such as string and toy as one.

Once a few of these simple, repetitive manipulative behaviour patterns are acquired, further questions arise concerning generalization of the behaviour patterns to other similar objects and the development of new patterns from existing ones. Again we lack data, apart from Piaget's, which include examples of the generalization of existing behaviour patterns to new, similar objects. Other observations suggest that new behaviour patterns are formed under two conditions. One is when there is feedback from an action that occurs by chance in the course of performing an existing behaviour pattern; for example, while the child is moving an object somewhere, he may happen to graze it on a rough surface, hear the new sound and acquire the behaviour pattern of rubbing objects on surfaces and producing a sound. The other condition is when an existing behaviour pattern is evoked by a new object for which it is inappropriate; a rattle with a flexible stem, that is fixed to a table, cannot, for instance, be picked up and shaken – if the child attempts to grasp it and as a consequence moves it and makes it sound, a pattern of patting the top or the stem may develop. [Piaget 1953 uses the term of 'assimilation' for the incorporation of a new object into an existing organized system, or 'schema', and the term of 'accommodation' for the modification of the action and the schema. New behaviour patterns (and learned schemata) develop from both processes.]

In addition to these behaviour patterns in which the same type of action is repeated, Piaget (1953) also suggests that the child from five or six months can learn to regulate the effort put into his action on the basis of the varying intensity of the resulting sound. His reported observations on this are not numerous, however, though he states that more instances of it occurred. A child of four months who could grasp objects he saw is reported to have learned to grade his movements when he was shaking a rattle, thereby varying the loudness of the sound (Ob. 106, O I).

We clearly need to know more about the development of such regulatory actions and with what level of organization they are associated. This brings us to the question of the interpretation of what the child of five to seven months has learned when he performs the manipulative behaviour patterns of shaking, patting, swinging, and so forth. When the child earlier lies in the pram and learns to shake himself and so produce events, all that is necessary for learning to occur is the association of the movement of shaking with the sensory event that follows it. Is this what is occurring in this and in the manipulative behaviour patterns? Has the child learned only a temporal relation between his action and the ensuing event or has he learned that his action produces the event? This discussion so far has been of actions that, in fact, produce events that lead to visual or auditory feedback. In order to answer the above question it is necessary to compare behaviour in this situation with the infant's behaviour when an event he perceives temporally follows an action of his, but is not caused by it. Behaviour in the second situation is discussed in the next section.

'Magical' actions

In the everyday situation the wind may move light toys, while the child is performing some action. This situation may be experimentally introduced if an investigator moves objects that the child is looking at or makes a sound. The following is an example from Piaget of the behaviour of a child aged eight months and nine days when he held a saucer in front of her and swung it. 'She looked at it and arched herself upwards, with her weight on her shoulder blades and feet and then fell in a heap. This was her usual reaction of pleasure. She repeated it when the saucer was passed in front of her again, several times.

Then the saucer was held still. She reacted with the arching and falling movement, as she continued to do whenever the saucer was held still' (Ob. 132, CR).

In this case the observer was in view, but Piaget reports that the same sort of behaviour occurred when he was out of sight and moved the objects hanging from the hood of the cot. The behaviour was thus not the result of social play, though this observation includes instances of such behaviour in relation to people when they sang and then stopped, and made sounds with objects and then stopped. In other instances the behaviour that is repeated is more complex. For example, Piaget reports that one of his daughters shook a bell that she held, after first trying other actions when he stopped imitating the mewing of a cat. He responded by making the sound again and then stopped; she again shook the bell (Ob. 113, OI). In this illustration the behaviour that is repeated itself produces an event from a different object, though this event is not the focus of the child's attention.

As far as is known to the writer, only Piaget has drawn attention to this behaviour of infants, though something analogous has been observed in other animals and has been termed 'superstitious behaviour' (Skinner, 1953). Piaget's interest was in the development of a 'practical understanding' of a causal sequence and he reports a number of observations of his children from the time they could grasp objects on visual contact to the age of about eight months, together with further observations of different behaviour between eight and eighteen months. But is it always an undirected movement that is conditioned to an event that is produced by some other agent? Or sometimes is the action that is repeated in this situation one that has already been associated with an event from an object? This is so, for example, if the child who has learned to shake himself in his pram and make hanging rattles swing performs the shaking action when someone stops singing. In this case a learned behaviour pattern is evoked. A possible explanation is that of generalization of the behaviour pattern from the first event, such as the sound of a hanging rattle, to any sound from any object, such as singing from a person. Piaget's interpretation is in terms of generalization, supported by a long series of observations. These begin with instances of the generalization of behaviour patterns, such as shaking or swinging objects that hang, to shaking or swinging new objects that can be grasped. They then go on to instances of the generalization of this kind of behaviour pattern to situations in which the child's action cannot produce the event from the object. The reader can find full details of these in observations 110 to 119 in OI and 128 to 140 in CR. Here a selection of them is made and briefly summarized.

One of them (Ob. 112, OI) is a further observation of the child aged three months who, earlier, had learned to grasp a chain or string and shake it so that a rattle attached to the other end swung and made a sound. A rubber doll was now tied to the near end of the string within reach of the child who grasped it and then sucked it for ten minutes. As the string was loose, the rattle did not move or make a noise. When the child dropped his hand from his mouth, while retaining the doll, Piaget moved the rattle and made it sound. The child looked at it, stretched out and shook his right arm, while still holding the doll. When he was no longer holding the doll, which was touching his right hand, Piaget shook the rattle again. The child reacted by moving his right arm without grasping the doll. The shaking arm action appears to have become differentiated from the 'pick up the string and shake it' sequence.

The rest of this series of observations demonstrates that the behaviour pattern of shaking the arm was subsequently evoked in a variety of situations. For example, a few weeks later the child shook his arm when his father stopped playing with him. A month later he waved his arm when a sound stopped (one made by Piaget when he was out of the child's visual field). When this child, at the age of nearly seven months, could not grasp an object that was too far away or could not make a distant object move, he shook his arm.

Another action performed by this child in this kind of situation was not differentiated from a causal one, as above, but was performed at once as a 'magical' action. The child was playing at striking a cushion with his hand when Piaget snapped his fingers. The child smiled and struck the cushion while looking at his father's hand. When the snapping sound did not recur, he struck the cushion harder and harder, 'with a definite expression of desire and expectation'. When Piaget began snapping his fingers again, the child stopped striking the cushion 'as though he had achieved his object'. This behaviour pattern was subsequently evoked when Piaget hid and reappeared from behind a curtain; it occurred also when he stopped switching an electric light switch on and off and when he stopped drumming on a tin box. This child also persistently struck the side of his cot and looked at the rattle that hung from it, and he struck the wrong end of his bottle, in the course of observations on 'the other side of the object' (Ob. 112 repeated, O I).

Another child, having learned to pull a string on the hood of her cot in order to swing things that were on it, performed this action when a variety of other objects were held still by her father at a distance, after he had moved them. This behaviour pattern appears to have been triggered off in the first place by the child's accidentally touching the string with her hand (Ob. 113, O I).

These observations of Piaget's, made some forty years ago, raise questions of such theoretical importance that further study of them is clearly necessary. These data suggest, for instance, that when an unfamiliar event occurs and then stops, children of five to eight months perform the action that preceded the event or perform one or more of their repertoire of existing behaviour patterns formed in relation to other objects. This suggests that the child's learning, when his action does produce the event, is also of the association between his action and the subsequent event. Comparisons of behaviour in these two situations of younger infants who cannot grasp objects on visual contact are needed. This is the kind of developmental question to which operant conditioning techniques could most usefully be applied.

Further studies are also needed on the extinction of the behaviour. Piaget's observations on this indicate that there is extinction on the specific occasion, but that the behaviour of reacting with magical procedures is remarkably persistent. He reports that when a particular action does not result in the recurrence of the event, it is performed less frequently on that particular occasion, but this does not prevent its being evoked on another occasion, along with a succession of other actions that have in the past been linked with the continuation of events. The child may run through his whole repertoire of actions that have previously produced events of any sort from objects. Sometimes he may have only a few at his disposal. One of Piaget's daughters, for instance, apart from sucking and grasping, had learned only the behaviour pattern of shaking her foot or body in order to make objects on her pram swing. When a new object was presented, she performed these three actions of shaking, sucking and grasping or attempting to grasp, alternately or simultaneously (Ob. 111, OI). In others the repertoire is larger. When Piaget drummed on a box and then stopped, his son clapped his hands, then waved goodbye with both hands, shook his head and arched upwards. This list is followed by 'etc.' (Ob. 134, CR).

There appears, from the evidence of these observations, to be a process of generalization which starts with similar events, such as sounds and movements from new objects in the same place as the original ones, or from new objects that can be held. But the generalization then appears to extend to objects in different places, to ones that are not held and to those at a distance, until finally any event from any object evokes in turn the whole repertoire of actions that have, in the past, been repeated since they preceded some such event. This is 'trial and error' behaviour, though each action that is tried, far from being any behaviour of the organism, is one that has been learned in relation to an external stimulus event. The persistence of this behaviour may be due to the fact that these actions do at times meet with success – when they do, in fact, produce events. This is a situation of intermittent reinforcement, which is conducive to slow extinction. The situation in which such intermittent reinforcement is most likely to occur is in social play: sometimes the adult will accede to the request to go on doing what he was doing and sometimes not. Smiling and various forms of protest may be the earliest behaviour patterns that are learned as producing 'events' from people.

Piaget reports that, with one child, he tried the experiment of no longer providing the event when the child performed the behaviour of arching herself. He introduced a variety of events once only, ranging from making the hood shake, to making vocal sounds himself and offering an object out of her reach. Each time, on numerous occasions over a period of a month, the arching action was performed (Ob. 132, CR).

It may even be the case that when he has the opportunity to act on the agent that produces the event, the infant does not do so in a way that lets it act, but tries to act on it himself. Piaget reports an interesting series of observations in which he gave his son aged seven months and seven days such an opportunity. He snapped his fingers and the child looked and laughed. He then repeated this, stopped and held his hand within reach of the infant, who grasped it and then struck it and shook it, rather than doing something such as giving it a push. 'He therefore treats it like a rattle whose properties depend on his own action and not at all like an independent source of activity' (Ob. 133, CR). When Piaget placed his hand thirty centimetres away, the child responded with some of his 'magical procedures', such as drawing himself up, and then, when the hand was within reach, he repeated the action of striking it and shaking it.

The same day Piaget drummed on a tin box that was just beyond the child's reach and he alternated between drumming and placing his hand, held still, within reach of the child, who smiled while the sound continued. When it stopped, the child clapped his hands, waved goodbye, shook his head, arched upward, and so on, while looking at the box – using his usual set of magical procedures. When his father's hand was placed near him, he twice took it, shook it and struck it, but did not move it towards the box (Ob. 134, CR).

A repetition immediately after this, with a toy that had movable parts, produced the same kind of reactions; it is reported, however, that the child visually followed his father's hand each time it left the toy and came towards him, though he quickly looked at the toy and adopted his 'magical' actions. On several occasions on the subsequent five days with a different object, the child behaved in the same way. On the fifth day the tin box was used again. If it was within his reach, the child took it when the drumming sound stopped, struck it and shook it, ignoring the hand. When the box was out of reach and the sound stopped, the child looked at the box, clapped his hands and drew himself up, etc.

This question certainly needs further investigation. If the child's learning in a situation in which his action *does* produce the event amounts to no more than the association of the temporal succession of action and event, is it an advance, as Piaget suggests, when the child responds to objects at a distance with an action that cannot possibly make the event occur again? Is it more advanced behaviour to run through the repertoire of learned behaviour patterns in response to *any* event from an object that is not near at hand than it is to perform the simple manipulative behaviour patterns discussed in the last section? It has already been argued that these manipulative behaviour patterns are more complex than the global bodily actions of shaking in a pram and so moving things that hang from it. The behaviour of waving an arm when an event occurs from an object at a distance may be equated with such global shaking actions and with actions that produce events from another part of the body, such as vocalization or movement of the hand. It would follow from this that the 'magical' actions are less complex than such behaviour patterns as banging a toy on a table and patting hanging objects. The basis for this distinction is not because in the latter case the action actually produces the event, whereas in the former it does not do so; it is because of the additional action of holding the object while performing actions upon it. There is, however, greater generalization in the case of the magical procedures, and for this reason Piaget considers they are an advance. The generalization appears to be that any visual or auditory event from any object evokes a behaviour pattern learned in relation to very different events and objects.

Possibly the advance is in the development of perception. No doubt, between the ages of two and eight months, the child's perception of his visual world has become more articulated and has extended to objects further away from himself. This may thus account for the generalization of behaviour patterns to events from more distant objects.

Is the performance of a succession of existing behaviour patterns, such as Piaget describes, more complex behaviour than the performance of one alone? The order in which a number of such behaviour patterns is performed is not crucial – as it is in the case of subsequent coordinated behavioural sequences. Hence, there is no basis for distinguishing a different level of behaviour on this count. More data are required before this question can be answered, particularly on the number of times the behaviour is repeated in the absence of the usual outcome. If each behaviour pattern is repeated fewer times when a succession of them is performed, compared with the number when one pattern alone is performed, the behaviour has changed. The change is abandoning more quicky behaviour that is not followed by the usual outcome. This would seem to be an advance.

A more important advance is when the child behaves differently when his actions have produced the events he perceives and when they have not. He behaves differently when he pushes an adult's hand towards the object from which it produced an event, and when he looks for a causal agent on seeing the movement of an object that he did not himself act upon.

Before going on to ask how the child gets beyond the use of magical procedures in these ways, we shall discuss other behaviour with similar features, occurring in the period before eight or nine months, to which Piaget has also drawn attention. This is the child's behaviour when objects come and go in different positions in space relative to the child and when an object, or one side of it, disappears from view altogether. Piaget reports (Ob. 72, CR) that the infant looks for people at the place where they came in and not where they went. He suggests that the child behaves as if the position of objects in space depended upon his actions. When an object falls from his grasp, the child makes a downward movement after it and retrieves it if it is in the path of this movement. This occurs only after grasping on sight has developed (Piaget, 1955; Woodward, 1959).

Objects that the child looks at, but has not recently held, may disappear from his visual field. An investigator may experimentally hide one by placing another object on top of the one the child is looking at. In this situation the child of six to seven months does not make a move to retrieve it, unless he has started moving his hand towards the object before it disappears from view. Woodward (1959) observed this behaviour in subnormal children who also retrieved objects they had just held, if they followed the path of the fall. Similar behaviour is reported to occur at this time with regard to one side of a single object. When he turned the nipple end of a feeding bottle away from the child, Piaget reports that the child did not rotate the bottle, although it was within his reach and he had just seen the nipple end.

In his very detailed discussions Piaget (1955) treats separately the infant's behaviour in relation to objects that go out of sight, his practical understanding of spatial relations and of causal sequences. The first two, at the time of 'magical' actions, can perhaps be regarded as further instances of the repetition of the action that was followed by an event from the object. Actions towards objects that are seen and those of moving down after objects that are falling from the hand are followed by the event of tactile contact with the object. The action of turning the head back to the position in space where an object was previously seen is followed by the event of seeing the object again. The trouble is that things do not always stay still in the same place: they move. As in the case of sounds and movements from the object that stays in view, movements of an object in and out of an individual's visual field, behind or under other objects, can be produced either by the action of the individual himself or by other agents. The same question is thus posed by the infant's behaviour in all these situations: how does he come to distinguish when his own action has produced the sound, the visible movement, the reappearance, and when some other causal agent has done so? Piaget's interpretation is that all these events are at first linked by the child to his own actions and that the distinction is made after a new development has taken place. This is the coordination of two behaviour patterns of the present phase. As he puts it somewhat colourfully, in a discussion of the child's behaviour when he sees objects disappear, the sensory image is at the 'disposal' of the child in somewhat the same way as an 'occult spirit is to the magician, ready to return if one catches it successfully but obeying no objective law' (Piaget, 1955, p. 13).

Coordination of behaviour patterns

Getting beyond 'magical' behaviour is thus a matter of the child's learning to distinguish between the outcomes of his own actions upon objects and those of other people or of inanimate forces; it also involves his distinguishing between reappearances of objects that are dependent on the movements of his head and those that are dependent on movements of the objects themselves.

What are the criteria for inferring that the child has made these distinctions? Behaviour of the child that has a different character is when he places the adult's hand back on the object it was producing an event from a short time ago, though Piaget (1955) maintains that with this the child is only partially transcending magical behaviour. This new behaviour has been reported by him to occur from the age of about eight months, along with different behaviour in problem situations that involve barriers, different manipulative behaviour with objects and different reactions to disappearing objects. In Piaget's view the type of behaviour pattern that is acquired during attempts to solve barrier problems is the important development that leads the child to begin to get beyond magical behaviour. The precise chronological sequence is not known in detail; further data are required for the full elucidation of this process. We may, however, examine the complexity of the various forms of behaviour to which Piaget (1953, 1955) has drawn attention, contrast them with previous behaviour and compare them with one another.

The behaviour in the problem situations is the following: when an obstacle, such as a low screen or an adult's hand, prevents the child from grasping an object that he can see, he eventually removes the obstacle, whereas previously he tried to move his hand over the top of it or round the side of it and did nothing more. Another example is pushing aside strings when a number of them are stretched across an object, for example, in a box. When an adult hangs on to a toy which is also held by the child, he pushes the adult's hand away, as he also does when an adult's hand holds his arm; previously he had tried to tug the toy free or struggled to free his arm. In the study of severely subnormal children, based on Piaget's work, the writer observed behaviour in these situations and found the above reactions. Piaget reports another instance of behaviour which he classifies as of the same type. This is more difficult to observe because of arranging the timing. The behaviour is putting down one object in order to take another. 'Putting down', with voluntary release, has to be distinguished from involuntary 'letting go'. The former entails the positive action of placing the object on something else, while dropping something is merely an action of release.

These are barrier situations. A different situation is when an adult stops what he is doing that entertains the child, such as singing or making a toy move or sound. When the child places the adult's hand back on the object, the behaviour is very different from that described in the last section. Also in contrast to earlier behaviour, though possibly a little later in appearing, is the child's removing, under certain conditions, the object that hides another that he saw go under it and turning round an object, thereby bringing into view the 'other more interesting side'. Different manipulative behaviour is alternately moving one object into different spatial positions and looking at it and turning one object round and round, while visually examining it. The writer has observed these manipulative behaviour patterns in children who could solve the simple barrier problems and not in those who could not.

Piaget (1953) has analysed behaviour in the solution of the barrier problems as the succession of two of the behaviour patterns of the previous period (his secondary circular reactions), carried out in a sequence such that the performance of the first allows the performance of the second. Pushing over an obstacle enables the child to grasp an object that is behind it. It is not always possible to observe the modification of an existing behaviour pattern into that of removing a barrier, though Piaget reports one such observation. The existing behaviour pattern was striking objects so that they swing. This pattern, applied to the barrier, eventually pushed the barrier over by chance. The second existing behaviour pattern of grasping the object could be performed once the barrier was removed. On subsequent occasions the coordinated sequence was performed once it had been carried out in the course of 'trial and error' action. This sequence is thus similar to behaviour of the previous period in that two existing behaviour patterns are evoked, but the order in which they are performed *does* matter; when the child runs through a succession of behaviour patterns in his repertoire when an event stops occurring, the order is irrelevant.

The important feature of these new coordinated sequences of behaviour, in contrast to those of a year later, is that they are acquired in the course of action, as the result of feedback from the accidental consequences of the performance of an existing behaviour pattern.

The solutions of other barrier problems may also be analysed as consisting of two existing behaviour patterns, which are performed in the correct sequence such that one is carried out in order to perform a second. Pushing an adult's hand off a toy and pushing aside string that holds an object in place are examples of such sequences. The previous behaviour of the single action of trying to tug the object loose was unsuccessful. The action of putting down one object in order to take another is equally a matter of carrying out one action in order to perform another.

Behaviour which at first glance appears different is when the child pushes an adult's hand off his arm. How can this be described as performing one action in order to perform another? If it is assumed that the adult's hand prevents a movement that would otherwise have occurred, the perform-ance of the movement is the second action which the perform-ance of the first allows.

When an adult stops doing something, the child is faced with a different problem: this is to take the action that will make the event occur again. In contrast to barrier situations, the solu-tion is to bring together the two objects, one of which pro-duced the event from the other. Examples are placing the hand of an adult on the object it was acting upon or touching the part of the body that produced the sounds, such as the lips. It may be noted that such actions do not necessarily produce the event; this depends upon the compliance of the adult with the request that is implied in the infant's action. The situation is thus different from that when only objects are involved; it may be more fruitful to look for the antecedents of this behaviour in the early social interactions of infant and adult rather than in the behaviour patterns of the child upon objects. This would direct attention to the cues given by the child which the adult interprets as signals to continue, start again or stop what he is doing.

Nevertheless, the behaviour upon the non-occurrence of an event is different from previous behaviour in such social situa-tions: the child appears to be transcending magical behaviour. He does not perform an irrelevant action. Moreover, the infant does not touch any part of the body of the adult who stops singing: he touches the lips. Similarly it is not any object that he places the adult's hand upon: it is that from which it was producing an event. From this we might suppose that the child has perceived a connection between the actions of other people upon objects and the events he sees and hears.

What has led to this? Looking at people and their actions in previous months may be a factor. From his early months the infant has been oriented towards the adult's face. This is near to him when an adult cares for him and plays with him. Eye-to-eye contact is reported by Wolff (1963) to be established by the end of the first month. Similarly the hands of adults are present in social play and in caretaking activities. Of all the objects in his environment that are separate from himself, the hands of other people are unique in that they have the same form as part of himself that he can see – his own hands. A recognition, first of the similarity and then of the difference between his own hands and those of other people, may thus be a necessary precursor to the behaviour being discussed. A possible contributing factor in this discrimination is the occurrence of kinaesthetic feedback from movement and holding actions with his own hands when he looks at them, which is not present when the hands of other people are regarded. People in the child's environment may thus be an essential factor in the process that results in the child's learning to distinguish when his own actions and when the actions of other agents have produced the events that he perceives.

Imitation of the manual actions of people may be a further factor. Imitation of movements and sounds has already begun before the period we are considering. The child who imitates a movement must look at the part of the body of the other person that is moving. The process leading to more exact imitation may direct attention towards the action of an adult upon an object.

Further, Piaget (1953) reports that his children developed a renewed interest in their hands before they began to solve the barrier problems. The children, at the age of seven or eight months, showed again the behaviour patterns typical of the third and fourth months: they looked at their hands for lengthy periods, twiddling their fingers or opening and closing the fist. As Piaget points out, it is likely that attention to some new feature about their hands has led to this renewed interest.

The interrelations between the social interactions of infant and adult and the development of more advanced behaviour patterns have still to be worked out. Schaffer and Emerson (1964) have drawn attention to the possible role of advances in behaviour in relation to disappearing objects and the formation of social attachments towards particular people. Such behaviour with regard to hidden objects, although an advance, reveals the limitations of the behaviour patterns of children of eight and nine months. It is from this that Piaget

(1953) argues that the infant at this time has only partially transcended magical behaviour.

The new behaviour is to look for an object that has gone out of sight. An observation of Piaget is particularly interesting in that it caught the development of the behaviour of uncovering an object. The child watched while a familiar toy was hidden under the edge of the cloth she was sitting on. She did not retrieve it. The next time the doll's feet were left protruding and she immediately pulled it out. The third time the doll was completely hidden again. The child 'pulls the cloth about and raises it as though she were discovering this new procedure in the very course of her groping, and perceives an extremity of the doll; she leans forward to see better, and looks at it much surprised. She does not grasp it.' Nor did she show any reaction of lifting the cloth on the fourth or fifth attempt. The sixth time the toy was hidden, she pulled the cloth about again, so that the object was visible. She 'again looks at it with great interest and at length, as though she did not recognize it. Then she grasps and sucks it.' The seventh time, she lifted the cloth at once, grasping both it and the toy together. On the last trial of this series of observations, she lifted the cloth at once, but nevertheless 'leaned forward in order to have a closer view of the doll before grasping it, as though she were not sure of its identity' (Ob. 38, CR).

The limitations of the retrieving behaviour, to which Piaget has drawn attention, is that the child of eight or nine months looks for the object on a second occasion in the place where he found it the first time. Piaget's attention was incidentally drawn to this phenomenon while a young nephew was staying in the house and was playing with a ball. The child retrieved the ball when it rolled under an armchair. When later it rolled under a sofa at the other end of the room, the child bent down to pull it out from under the sofa, but he persisted only for a moment and looked for it under the armchair (Ob. 52, CR). This led Piaget to study this behaviour systematically in his own children.

His technique was to show the child an object, hide it under one cover (A) and let the child retrieve it. He then took the object and while the child was looking hid it under a second cover (B) in a different place. For example, the child quoted above was shown a different cover being slowly lowered on to the doll at the place about ten centimetres from that previously used. Although she could easily have reached it, she whimpered for a while, but did not look for it. When it was placed under the first cloth, she found it at once, but when it was placed under the new cover again, on three subsequent trials, she lifted the original cloth (Ob. 38, CR). In subsequent observations the object was alternately hidden under cover A and cover B or was placed under each several times in succession. Two of Piaget's children did not once look under cover B, though the third one did so intermittently. Between the ages of nine months, seventeen days and nine months, twenty-eight days this third child looked under cover A every time an object was hidden under it, while he looked under cover B on only six of the thirty-two occasions that an object was hidden there.

Apart from Piaget's detailed observations (Obs. 34–52, CR), there has been little study of behaviour in this situation. The writer found little evidence of the behaviour among subnormal children, though the reason may be that the phase is a brief one and hence not found in many of a large group observed only two or three times. Luria (1959), however, reported similar behaviour in slightly older infants (twelve to fourteen months), with regard to verbal behaviour. Two equally attractive toys, a fish and a horse, were placed in front of the child, who was requested three or four times to give the experimenter the fish, which he did. Then he was asked to hand over the horse (a word he knew) and again the fish was given.

Piaget's observations, made at frequent intervals over a period of a few weeks, contain several suggestions for further inquiry, with the benefit of modern recording equipment.

For example, Piaget reports of one child that she looked under the cover where she first found the object, even though the object was left in view. The first cover was her father's hand, placed on the toy on her lap. When the toy was on the table and the hand on her lap, as before, she is reported to have looked at the object while lifting the hand (Ob. 39, CR).

Secondly, he reports that a sound coming from a masked object, in this period, is no more effective in directing the child's search away from the place where he first found the object. (It will be remembered that the child looks in the direction of a sound in his third month.) The writer's findings provide partial support for Piaget's observation on this point. The object was not first shown and hidden. It was presented already under a cloth and then made to sound; children who removed the cloth when they heard the sound had acquired the more advanced behaviour patterns to be described in the next chapter.

Piaget's interpretation of this behaviour is that the child is still behaving as if the objects he sees and their positions in space depend upon his own actions – in other words, his learning is still only of the connection between the action and the sensory event that follows it. In this connection it is of interest that 'hiding and finding games' are common at this period. Children repetitively lift a cover such as the corner of a blanket, look at an object under it, cover it up again, uncover it and so on. Although the structure of the behaviour has the same form as removing a screen and taking an object under it, this behaviour is somewhat different from retrieving an object that has been hidden by someone else or one that rolls out of sight. In covering and then uncovering an object, the child is repeating his own action and he has made the object disappear from view himself. He is thus performing actions that are followed by events: lifting the cloth makes the object come into view, putting it down makes it disappear. For months before this children have had the experience of turning their head back to the position they have just been in and seeing again the object they were looking at before – if it remains in the same place. It would not be surprising, therefore, if these two kinds of experience have led the child to associate the re-appearance of an object with an action of his own.

It might be expected that children who find an object that has gone out of sight under a cover would also turn a single object round when the significant side has been turned away from them. Piaget (1955) reports observations to this effect, together with the new manipulative behaviour pattern of turning an object round and round and looking at its different sides. The writer found a correspondence between this manipulative behaviour and solution of simple barrier problems (Woodward, 1959).

Piaget further reports other manipulative behaviour with a single object: the child holds the object alternately close to his face and at arm's length, while looking at it, and holds it at different angles. Piaget (1955) discusses this behaviour in relation to the development of size and shape constancy. Direct studies of the perceptual constancies in infancy, however, yield ambiguous results (Wohlwill, 1960).

Behaviour that is similar to manipulating a single object and changing its position in relation to the self is that of moving the head or body and getting different views of a stationary object. Piaget reports that one child moved his head and looked, raised himself or bent over the edge of the cot and looked. Such action and the visual feedback from this, together with those of moving the single object and getting visual feedback of different views, may provide the experiences that enable the child to sort out when objects are moving and when he is. This is what Piaget suggests is occurring at this time and he cites in support of this view the difference in the speed of the head movements, compared with earlier ones. He reports that the head movements of the third to seventh month are rapid shakes without pauses in between; these are interpreted as magical actions. The infant of eight to ten months, in contrast, is reported to pause and look after each of these head movements. Again time measures of the intervals between movements and records of eye movements are needed in order to follow up these reported differences in behaviour.

If confirmed, this difference might very well be the important distinguishing feature between the less advanced and more advanced behaviour patterns of the first ten months. To pause and look after each action of shaking is to get visual feedback of the outcome of each *specific* action. When the infant swings an object or shakes a rattle, the continuing movement or sound *accompanies* the *continuing* action. Moreover, to pause and look is *active*. Piaget reports instances of pausing and looking in manipulative behaviour too. He distinguishes behaviour patterns which he terms 'derived secondary circular reactions', classifying them as secondary reactions because the same kind of action is repeated; the difference that Piaget stresses is that the child appears to be trying to 'find out' about the object, rather than just to reproduce the event. An example is the following. A child picked up a hanging chain, shook it, let go and then paused and watched the movement before swinging it again. Shaking has to be withheld while the movement is watched. In this respect, therefore, these behaviour patterns are similar to the behavioural sequence when the child removes a barrier and grasps an object, and when he places an adult's hand where it can act. They, too, may be interpreted as the coordination of two existing behaviour patterns of turning to look at stationary or moving objects and of repeating the action that produced the event, without pausing in between to look. The pausing and looking in the head-shaking reported by Piaget may also be distinguished from turning to look successively at different objects or alternately between two. In the latter case one object at a time is looked at. If Piaget's interpretation of the later, slower head-shaking is correct, the pausing and looking is at *relations* among objects, of the changed spatial relations that result from different positions of the head.

Such pauses between actions point the way to the development of behavioural sequences in which each action is slightly modified on the basis of the outcome of the preceding action; such sequences are the subject of the first part of the next chapter. The second part deals with problem-solving behaviour which is the first kind to qualify for a description as 'thinking'. Pausing after acting to look and listen, instead of looking and listening while acting, may very well be the beginnings, at a sensorimotor level, of reflection, of stopping to think.

4 Looking Ahead

The behaviour patterns to be examined first in this chapter, although more complex than those treated so far, still have the feature that feedback from a chance-made action leads to the repetition of that action. Their continuity with the previous ones is thus fairly clear. In the case of those to be considered in the second part of this chapter, there appears to be a greater difference and the process by which they develop out of previous ones is not clearly understood. These are problem-solving actions of the type that have been termed 'insightful' or 'cognitive'. Associated with these are such developments as the completion of the 'object concept' and other behaviour which refers to objects not perceptually present. A further concurrent development with these, during the second year, is that of language. This raises the question of the relation of this to the cognitive developments.

The first type of different behaviour patterns begins before the end of the first year (Lézine, Stambak and Casati, 1969). They include the solution of problems by taking account of the spatial relation of two objects. Examples of such problems are those in which an object is out of the child's reach, standing upon a supporting object or attached to a string which can be pulled in order to draw the object near. The manipulative behaviour patterns are ones that produce variations in sounds and movements and that alternately arrange and disarrange objects in various spatial relations in, alongside or upon.

Variation on a theme

The manipulative behaviour patterns that produce sounds and movements have two new features, which Piaget (1953) distinguished. In some, the chance-made movement that is repeated has to be more precise for the same outcome to be produced; consequently it is more difficult for the child to 'find' it again. For example, in order to make an object lift up by pressing on it, pressure on any part of it will not produce a repetition of the event of tilting; it is necessary to press on a specific part. The other new feature of these behaviour patterns is that, once the action is repeated, further performances are variations of the action and the event produced by it; this is in contrast to the repetition of the same kind of event in previous behaviour patterns. For example, an object is banged successively on different surfaces instead of on the same one. An object is dropped into water from different heights, pushed along or held down in the water, released and allowed to bob up again. Other behaviour patterns are rolling and spinning objects, letting them slide and pouring water. Piaget (1953), who drew specific attention to these behaviour patterns, terms them 'tertiary circular reactions'. Although a succession of actions that is a variation on a theme is manifestly different from the successive repetition of the same action, there are some common components in the two sequences. When, for instance, an object is banged on either the same surface or a succession of different ones, the upward and downward movements in the banging action are similar. The difference lies in the interpolated movement to a different object before banging it in the second case. This movement is followed by halting above the surface, bringing the object to it and hearing a sound which is different from the last one. When an object is dropped in succession from different heights, the upward movement has to be longer or shorter than before. When a ball is rolled further, it has to be pushed harder. It is the movement to a different surface or to a different height, etc., that has to be accounted for. The visual or auditory feedback, instead of being a condition for the repetition of the action that produced it, is a condition for the performance of a variation of it.

Studies such as the writer's, that observe whether or not the behaviour patterns are in the child's repertoire, are unlikely to provide an explanation of this. Further intensive study of the process by which the behaviour patterns are acquired is necessary for such an explanation, as it is also for the elucidation of how the child comes to repeat a more precise chance-made action. Piaget's observations are again suggestive concerning the process by which a child arrives at more precise action. For example, one child had dropped an unfamiliar object – a round, flat box. While she was trying to pick it up, she accidentally pressed the edge. This had the result that the box was tilted up and then fell again. The child apparently observed this event. Attempts to make the event occur again were at first unsuccessful; the action of pressing the box was evoked, but the precise place had to be found. She pressed it in the middle instead of the edge. This made the box slide, and she was diverted to playing at making it slide, before she returned to pressing the box. A chance press on the edge produced the tilting and falling result. She then continued to press the box on the edge, repeating this action and the event, with variations (Ob. 146, O I).

Both the similarity and the difference, when compared with the previous form of behaviour pattern, emerge in this example. A new event results from an attempt to do something else and the action that produced it is repeated; this is similar. Discovering the action is more difficult: the action has to be more precise for the event to be reproduced, and the first attempt fails; this is different. A sequence of actions, each of which is a slight modification of the previous one, has also a different character from a sequence that is repeated without much variation. In this new behaviour pattern the child appears to be performing variations on a theme or extrapolating from the original action. It may be postulated that the process of finding the action that produced the event is one of the successive modification of each action on the basis of feedback of the outcome of the previous one. Piaget maintains that the variation on a theme sequence occurs by means of this process too.

In another example he suggests that the child is comparing the different sounds when he bangs objects on different surfaces. This hypothesis is more difficult to test. The observation in question does, however, illustrate another point. A pattern of varied banging was triggered off by an unexpected event – the usual outcome of an action did not occur. The action was pulling, but the object pulled was the circular tier of a table on a pivot, which moved round instead of towards the child. He shook it, knocked it and then struck it several times with varying effort, thus varying the sound. He then alternated between this and striking his own table. Piaget inferred from the child's behaviour that he was comparing the sounds. The child then alternately struck the tier of the table and a chair (Ob. 143, O I).

That the child is comparing two different sounds or sights is perhaps a reasonable inference from the behaviour just described. If one action with a certain outcome leads to the modification of the next action, with a different outcome and so on, successive outcomes may be compared. In the last chapter attention was drawn to Piaget's suggestion that the infant of nine or ten months has begun to compare the different spatial relations of objects when his head is in different positions and when he looks at the result of one manipulative action upon one object. These may be regarded as of a higher level than the simpler secondary circular reactions, which continue a sound or movement without the pause. The behaviour patterns just described may be regarded as of a higher level still. The comparison of two different events, following two different actions upon objects, is inferred, instead of the comparison of different results upon stationary objects achieved by movement of the body alone. Changing the spatial relations of objects by moving the objects themselves may also be regarded as more complex than moving the body. Manipulation that achieves this will be considered after a discussion of problem solving in which the solution requires the recognition of the spatial relation of two objects. These are problems of objects out of reach, upon or attached to another object.

The behaviour patterns that are variations on a theme do not have an end-result that is to be achieved, as barrier problems have, though finding precisely what to do in order to make an event occur again may perhaps be regarded as a problem. In this case the end-result towards which the actions are directed is not perceptually present. In the case of problems of objects out of reach, the object towards which the actions are directed is in view. But if the actions are made directly towards it, the problem cannot be solved; the solution consists in directing action towards another object, the string or support, and first pulling this.

The study of 'string problems' was begun with monkeys and children many years ago. Complex problems involving several strings but with an object on only one of them were often used. In the study of development, we are concerned with the acquisition by children for the first time of the behaviour pattern of using a support or string in order to pull an object near – in the simplest form with one string or support presented. An additional one is useful at this point only in order to check whether the child perceives the relations of the object to support or string. That he does this and pulls the support or string after seeing the object move, as the result of moving the support or string by chance, is essential for the classification of the behaviour into this different category. If the child gives up attempts at direct grasping and is diverted to play with the objects within reach, fortuitously obtaining the object as a result of shaking or grasping the string or support, the behaviour is of the same type as that discussed in the last chapter. In the observation of this behaviour it is, of course, necessary to devise procedures for finding out which it is. Two overlapping supports may be presented, with the object on the one that is further away from the child. If he stops pulling the nearer one when the object does not move with it and then grasps and pulls the other support, there is evidence that the child is observing the related movements of the two objects and that this observation guides his behaviour. Similarly, two overlapping strings may be presented, only one being attached to the object.

Once the child has observed the result of moving the string or support, his problem then is to pull both in the correct direction towards himself. Piaget (1953) suggests that this also is achieved by a process of successive modification by regulatory visual feedback; if one action pushes the toy further away, the next action is in a different direction. He points out, however, that the succession of movements is too rapid for a human observer to record them and film records are necessary for the details of the process to be known.

When the behaviour pattern has been acquired, the smoothed performance is observed: the child grasps the string or support and pulls it in a straight line towards himself and grasps the object. With only three exceptions in a group of sixty-five subnormal children, the writer found that either both the string and support patterns were present or both were absent. Children who solved these problems removed a screen in order to obtain the object behind it. Lézine, Stambak and Casati (1969) report that the string and support behaviour patterns were present towards the end of the first year.

If these behaviour patterns are acquired by a process of regulatory feedback, such as Piaget suggests, it would be expected that the manipulative behaviour patterns that have been described would develop at around the same time. Moreover, since these problems involve the spatial relation of one object upon another, it would not be surprising if children who have acquired the behaviour patterns of the support and string were found to manipulate objects in a way that placed them upon, in and alongside one another. Woodward (1959) found such a correspondence in about half her cases. The exceptions were, however, mainly one way round: the higher level manipulative behaviour patterns were frequently absent among children who solved the string and support problems, though they were rarely present among children who did not. There were many instances of behaviour disturbances in the group (see Woodward, 1960 and 1963 for a description) and this was significantly more common among the cases of non-correspondence between problem solving and manipulative behaviour patterns than among those of correspondence. The discrepancy may thus be attributed to the higher motivation to obtain a valued object in the problem situation than to 'explore' new objects.

When the child at this period has a scattered group of

about a dozen small objects, he does not put them all into different spatial relations, on top of, beside or in others. He takes a few, arranges them, disarranges them, arranges them again, and so on. For example, a few objects from the collection are placed in and out of a hollow container. In this behaviour the child is reproducing the same arrangement, rather than varying it. The result of his action is, however, more complex than obtaining a sound from repeatedly banging an object on the same surface. Several objects and a spatial relation among them is involved and the action that reproduces the result is more complex than those that produce an event from a single object, such as swinging or banging. In these cases the second object has a subsidiary role. In order to repeat the action, of putting objects in, upon or beside others, the child has first to undo what he did. In these behaviour patterns the feedback of the result of the action, the changed spatial arrangement, thus appears to be a condition for reversing the action, of undoing the arrangement and then repeating it. The writer (Woodward, 1959) found this behaviour pattern among children who solved the string and support problems.

We may ask now why these and other behaviour patterns that have been discussed were not developed earlier. Ever since children could grasp on sight, the problem of objects out of reach has existed and objects could have been spun, put in others, dropped in water, banged on various surfaces, and so forth. The point is that they were not.

With regard to the manipulation of objects, it seems highly probable that the more complex actions and events occurred once by chance in previous months. If so, it may be feedback from the events that did not occur and so an attempt to repeat the action was not made. Alternatively, the child may have seen the event, but could repeat only the global action and could not go through the process of successive modification to find the precise action. The kind of manipulative development described at the end of the last chapter may be a necessary precursor. The particular example given was holding and shaking a chain, and pausing and watching the movement before shaking again. The important prior development may be pausing after an action and observing the result. This may lead to the comparison of two successive events that arise from a chance variation in the action and so to the development of the pattern of successive variation. Again, timed records of the action and intervals between them would be useful, together with records of the direction of the child's glance. If there is comparison of two succeeding sounds or movements, this makes the behaviour patterns that produce such events comparable to those that reproduce the same spatial relation as before: in one case the child is relating temporal events, in the other spatial arrangements.

In both cases, however, the temporal integration of successive events and actions is involved: two different actions, one a modification of the other, are performed and the two outcomes are compared, the whole sequence being integrated over time. This is a more complex sequence to be integrated than that of removing an obstacle and grasping the object behind it. The obstacle has only to be removed by knocking or pushing; the outcome of a sound or movement does not have to be observed and compared with the outcome of grasping the object. Nor does the spatial relation of obstacle to object have to be observed and used to guide the next action, as it does in the case of repeating the action of placing one object in or upon another.

Hebb (1966) has made the point that temporal integration is one of the most important features of the behaviour of higher animals in a waking state and that this presupposes immediate memory, which 'makes it possible to coordinate past experience and action with future action' (p. 291). The infant, towards the end of his first year, appears to have made advances in such integration, though an inference that the infant 'anticipates' a future action at this period may be questioned.

A memory factor may also be involved when it takes some time to 'find' the action that produced an event that was observed. While the infant 'tries' various actions, that event is presumably held in some way. In infancy, however, it is not necessarily held by a central mediating process of the kind

Hebb means. It may be held by an action. Some of the behaviour that led Bruner (1968) to this interpretation has already been described. Another situation in which it was observed was when the infants were faced with a difficult reaching problem; they kept their mouths open and hands unfisted while performing the reaching action. Bruner terms this 'place-holding' and interprets the behaviour as a strategy of action for keeping the end-result of grasping and sucking in view while the intermediate action is performed. The infants discussed by Bruner were younger (six to seven months) than those whose behaviour is being analysed at present. Nevertheless the same principle may apply. Further research is necessary to determine whether strategies of action (place-holding) or a memory factor enter into these more complex behaviour patterns – and into the earlier ones of removing obstacles too.

Some such word as strategy seems to be necessary for distinguishing this kind of behaviour, involving two simultaneous actions, from that in which a single action is performed in a stimulus situation. The use of the term 'strategy' should not necessarily be taken to imply cognitive processes beyond the level of a sensorimotor sequence. Similar caution needs to be exercised in the use of the word 'understanding' to refer to interpretations of the behaviour of infants in their first year.

Piaget (1953) has made the point that the main difference between these behaviour patterns (his tertiary circular reactions) and the earlier secondary ones is that the child tries to analyse and understand rather than merely to reproduce events. Such 'analysis' and 'understanding', at this period of development, can only mean more complex feedback loops – observation by the child of the outcome of his own action, which guides the next one.

The new behaviour patterns are, however, much less limiting than the previous ones. These earlier ones were formed by learning to repeat an action that by chance produced an event. The capacity to acquire a large collection of such behaviour patterns has its limitations, from the point of view of gathering information about new objects or new features of familiar objects. The event has first to occur from a chance-made action. Modification of behaviour patterns can occur only within this circuit: in the course of attempting to perform an action that cannot be performed in the situation, another action and consequent event occur accidentally and this action is repeated. The two actions and events are separate; there is no necessary interrelating by the child of one to the other; repetition of the second results from the chance outcome of it, upon the non-occurrence of the usual outcome of the first action. When, on the other hand, the new event that occurs is a slight variation on the previous one that *did* occur, we might infer that the actions and outcomes are connected by the child. Thus, the production of novel events, by minor variations on a theme, is an advance on the earlier manner of performing the action that produces a new event. Since the other new feature is observation of the results upon one object of moving another, developments in visual following may be a condition for the development of these new behaviour patterns or a contributory factor in it. Such visual following may also contribute to the change in the child's behaviour when an object is hidden, to his search in the place where he saw it hidden, rather than where he previously found it. Visual following of the actions of other people upon objects and observation of the sequence of the action and the event may play a part in the child's behaviour with regard to the movement of objects. The actions of spinning and rolling objects, pushing them down in water and letting them bob up again, pushing them in water and letting them float and letting them slide down slopes have already been mentioned. All of these actions place the object in a situation in which it then moves, without the continued intervention of an action by the child. Thus it would seem that the child has learned that some events are not produced by his actions. When the usual outcome does not occur, the child now varies his action, instead of running through his repertoire of behaviour patterns that are inappropriate in the situation. If the toy does not slide down a slope, he places it on different materials with sloping surfaces. But having learned that some things will slide, the child is faced with the further problem of learning when they do, if placed in a certain position, and when a push is necessary as, for instance, when a ball is placed on the floor. Piaget claims, too, though it is difficult to observe the difference, that the child goes for several weeks behaving as if his action of throwing is necessary to the fall: he throws objects, does not let them fall as he does when he lets an object slide down a slope.

The converse of perceiving the spatial relations of objects to one another is to place them in such relations: in, upon, next to, behind, etc. We do not know whether one leads to the development of the other or whether there is an interactive process, with a development in perception contributing to the acquisition of new forms of behaviour patterns which in turn contribute to further perceptual developments, and so on. Piaget infers from the child's alternately arranging objects into certain spatial relations and disarranging them, that the child is finding out about the spatial relations of objects to one another. The question of the relations between visual following, perception of events, actions and spatial relations, and the acquisition of behaviour patterns, requires further study before it can be answered.

Piaget (1953) has drawn attention to an interesting point which also merits further investigation. This concerns the way the child relates different parts of an object that is too large to be seen all at once. He reports an observation of his son who was sometimes given a long stick to play with, between the ages of twelve to sixteen months. On one occasion, he pushed the stick in all directions, apparently watching the movement of one end that resulted from his actions in moving the other end, and he ran his eye down the length of the stick (Ob. 177, O I). When objects such as sticks are being moved about, they are likely to chance to move another object at times. When the event is observed and the action repeated and varied, as with other manipulative behaviour patterns of this period, the behaviour comes close to the tool using which is regarded as one mark of the higher animal. This behaviour pattern, observed by Piaget, may be a precursor to the use of instruments in the problem situations considered in the next section.

Foresight

The differences between the behaviour patterns discussed in this chapter and the last have been emphasized up to this point. Now the similarities will be stressed when all of these types of behaviour pattern are contrasted with another type in a certain problem situation. The problem situation is one in which the subject has the opportunity to perform a sequence of actions in the correct order for a successful outcome without first having observed the outcome of that particular sequence of actions. This may be contrasted with a solution achieved in the course of action in a problem situation, after a longer sequence of 'trial and error' actions, when the smoothed performance is arrived at *after* the solution is achieved and *after* the outcome of the action has been seen.

The kinds of problem situations which allow the above distinction to be made are those devised by Köhler (1925) in his classic study of apes. Examples are an object out of reach and a stick within reach which can be used to pull in the object (direct locomotion to the object being prevented), or an object above the subject to which he can pull a box or a stool.

The performance of a correct sequence of actions before the outcome is seen has been termed 'insightful problem solving', though it has been noted, before now, that 'foresight' might be a more accurate description. Complex human thinking provides many examples of the anticipation of the outcomes of actions and of prior central events without overt action. We are thus concerned with the development of the early forms of thinking.

Much argument about the interpretation of insightful problem solving followed the work of Köhler and others. It is not proposed to enter into this here, since much of the dispute has been about problem solving in the rat and ape – though the evolution of complex behaviour is of interest. The importance of the beginning of this kind of problem solving in human development is that it raises the question of a new principle, of central mediating processes, or thinking. It is the explanation of the development of these first forms of thinking from earlier behaviour patterns that is important for those who seek the explanation of human thinking from overt behaviour and sensory feedback. It may then be less of a problem to explain how more complex forms develop from these.

Current controversies tend to centre around the nature of the central mediating processes, rather than to argue about their role. For instance, both Berlyne (1965) and Miller, Galanter and Pribram (1960), from different theoretical positions, pointed out that, whatever rats and apes may or may not do, people do anticipate the results of actions before they are performed. Some of the earlier arguments were concerned with the issue of whether or not past experience is necessary for the solution. From the developmental perspective, we are interested both in past experience and in how it is reorganized. As hitherto in this discussion, we shall ask of what existing behaviour patterns do new, more complex ones consist? We are now, however, posing a new question in addition: how does the child come to select and combine existing components and arrange the order in which they are to be performed, before he has performed the actions in that order? Previously we have asked how, in the course of action, the child arrives at the sequences which solve the problem concerned.

Consider the problem of the stick and object out of reach, in this light. First the sequence has to be described more precisely than using a stick to pull an object near. Omitting lower level actions such as grasping the stick and the object, the behaviour is placing the stick in the spatial relation to the object that is necessary for pulling the object nearer and then performing the action of pulling the object with the stick, so that the object comes within reach. One of the two component behaviour patterns, from among those already discussed, is thus arranging and disarranging objects in certain spatial relations to one another; the second is moving one object with another in various directions. If the child solves the stick problem with precision, he has to place the stick in a specific spatial relation to the object, behind it, and he has to pull the object with the stick, in a specific direction, towards himself. This means that the selection of the spatial relation in the first action is determined by the nature of the second action. The first action is performed in such a way that the second can then be performed. The whole sequence of actions is thus a coordinated one; if this sequence is performed without error on the first occasion, the coordination is achieved prior to the performance and prior to the observation of the outcome of it.

Contrast this with the behaviour of attempting to grasp the object directly, then picking up the stick, moving it in various ways, accidentally displacing the object with it, one way or another, observing the outcome of the action and, as a consequence, modifying the direction of the next displacement, until finally the stick is placed behind the object and is used to pull the object into reach. When the coordination is achieved prior to the performance of the sequence of actions, the question of mediating processes is raised, in order to account for the inferred combining combining of elements of past experience in a new way.

A sharp distinction has just been made between two ways of arriving at the efficient sequence of actions for solving a problem. One is by selecting and arranging the order before any action is performed; the other is by arriving at the selection and arrangement in the course of experience with the particular problem. This should not be taken to imply that children in practice move abruptly from one to the other. The distinction, with the strict criterion of errorless performance on the first occasion, is made for purposes of analysis; it is made in order to contrast the problem solving of the young infant, which can be interpreted in terms of action and sensory feedback alone, with some problem solving of human adults, who indubitably are able to anticipate the consequences of actions before they perform them, on the basis of prior 'thinking' processes, of selecting from and combining units of past experience, in relation to the problem as given.

These ways of solving problems have sometimes been characterized as overt and as implicit trial and error. Whether or not children achieve this prior selecting and sequencing during their second year is a less important point than the fact that they do at some time during their development. The first step is to define the two kinds of problem solving; the next is then to seek to elucidate the process of change from one to the other.

The important distinction is prior selecting and sequencing rather than precise, errorless solution. If children show evidence of this 'foresight' with one problem, it may be postulated that they would do so with other problems that are of similar complexity, provided that the behaviour for solution consists of components that have already been performed. If, on the other hand, children manage to solve one of these problems by observation of the chance result of an action, followed by repetition of it, with variations, it may be postulated that they would solve other different ones in the same way: the correct action would have first to occur by chance and its outcome be observed. In the study of these questions it is clearly necessary to distinguish between the opportunity of children to learn the component behaviour patterns, on the one hand, and, on the other, the opportunity to attempt to solve the specific problem whose solution is achieved by the combination of these components. It is one thing to have the opportunity to handle a group of objects and a stick; it is another to be presented frequently with the situation of an object out of reach and a stick within reach.

The ideal situation for finding out whether or not children can perform a coordinated sequence of actions without having seen the outcome of a previously combined performance of them, is to present the problem to children who are known to have had no opportunity for long practice at attempting to solve it. The problem may then be presented at infrequent intervals and the manner of solution, when it appears, may be compared with that of children of the same age given practice and demonstration. Unfortunately most investigators do not know much about the everyday life of the children they study – whatever the disadvantages of parent-investigators, they can control the environment of the child in this way.

Once more Piaget's observations give us most detail on this question.

He gave two of his children many opportunities to tackle the stick and toy out of reach problem from the age of twelve months, and the third was presented with it infrequently. One of the first two eventually learned to solve it through what appeared to be a process of visual feedback from chance-made actions and the further modification of these actions when repeated, as in the acquisition of the string and support patterns, until a smooth performance was achieved. The other was at one point given the opportunity to observe the correct action; she then imitated it. The object was a cork on a table and the child was handed the stick after she had seen the demonstration. She imitated the action and the cork fell. But on a subsequent occasion she tried to grasp the cork directly, and used the stick only when it was placed in her hand, though after several trials it was sufficient for an adult to point to the stick and eventually she picked it up without being shown it first. She did not, however, succeed in using a stick in order to pull an object towards her when the object was out of reach on the floor. She merely touched the object with the stick. Two months later, at the age of fifteen-and-a-half months, the object on the floor moved slightly when she struck it. This she observed and pushed the toy with the stick until she could grasp it (Obs. 159–61, OI).

The important feature of this behaviour, which certainly requires further study in children of one to one-and-a-half years, is that the *specific* behaviour that was learned in one situation was performed in a different one in which it was inappropriate. The specific behaviour pattern of *hitting* an object with a stick had been learned, since it resulted in making an object on a table fall to the ground. The behaviour that was repeated was that which previously led to the outcome that had been observed. Thus it would seem that observation of the action of another person is insufficient for prior appropriate sequencing in a different situation.

The results of Lézine, Stambak and Casati (1969) confirm the observation on imitation. They found that the behaviour of pulling an object with a stick after demonstration or after trial and error action both occurred in their fifteen to eighteen months group, along with the behaviour of pushing one object with a stick. Solution without a demonstration or trial and error occurred more often in the group aged fifteen to twenty months, together with the solution to a similar problem that was used by Piaget, of getting a chain out of a matchbox.

A problem that involves only one component action and one 'anticipated' outcome of a change in spatial relations appears to be solved before one that requires the combination of two, such as the stick problem. An example of the former is the problem of a long toy presented horizontally on the other side of vertical bars; the toy has to be rotated ninety degrees to be parallel with the bars. Some children try to tug the toy through without changing its position. The writer (Woodward, 1959) found that some subnormal children solved this problem by quickly rotating the toy, while being unable to solve the stick problem, though the converse was not found.

Although further data are required concerning the process by which this change occurs, we may nevertheless proceed to analyse the development of the ordering of a sequence of actions prior to their performance. In order to do this, we need a term for the stored sensorimotor units that have been learned through interactions with the environment. So far 'behaviour pattern' has served, since we have dealt with sequences of action that have been evoked by stimulus situations with which they have been associated; modification of the action has occurred from the child's observation of the outcome of it. It has been necessary to refer only to the pattern of action and feedback and not to the stored unit. When we discuss manipulation before action of such stored units of past transactions with the environment, we need a term by which to refer to them. The term 'schema', as proposed by Bartlett (1932), will be used; this is 'an active organization of past reactions or past experience'. We may thus describe as a schema the neural changes that occur in the learning of a pattern of action such as striking hanging objects and producing a movement that is seen. This is a sensorimotor schema that relates a certain action to a certain class of objects and events. Similarly we may speak of verbal schemata. In his early writing Piaget, too, (see e.g. 1953, 1955) used the term 'schema' in a similar sense, though he now distinguishes 'schemata' and 'schemes' (Piaget 1968).

The question of the arranging of sensorimotor schemata before they issue into action takes us on to a discussion of plans as processes that may achieve this and of the associated question of what is often termed 'representation'.

Plans and representation

The stick and object out of reach problem will still be used for purposes of analysis, though any similar ones would do. It has been suggested that the two components are selected and sequenced in the appropriate order for the attainment of the end-result of grasping the object that is out of reach. To grasp the stick and perform a pulling action with it, without first placing it behind the object, would be inappropriate, as would trying to grasp the object before grasping the stick.

It has further been suggested that one of the component schemata is placing one object near another, with the out-come that the spatial relation between the two objects is changed; the other is moving one object with the other, with the result that the distance between the child and the object that was out of reach is decreased. Each of these two larger segments consists at the lower levels of such small segments as grasping the stick, pushing it in the correct direction towards the object and placing it behind the object; these smaller segments, for example, grasping the stick, could be broken down into their component smaller parts, and so on. The essential point is that the smallest segments have already been combined earlier in development and the resulting combinations have also been combined; furthermore, the behaviour of correcting movements of an object in the wrong direction is assumed also to have been already learned, so that a smoothed performance may be executed. A developmental analysis such as this thus postulates that it is these larger units that are evoked by the problem situation and sequenced, rather than the smaller segments from which they have been developed. The schema of grasping objects is a lower level part of the first of these components. It then occurs as a separate action, after the object has been brought within reach, when that object is grasped.

A postulate of the prior sequencing of sensorimotor schemata requires explanation of what prevents the schemata that are evoked from issuing into action. One means by which action is prevented is negative social reinforcement, but that does not apply in this case. The end-result towards which the sequence of actions is directed in the stick problem is grasping the object that is out of reach. This schema is presumably evoked by the situation; if attempts at direct grasping are not made, it must be assumed that they are withheld. Learning from previous experience can account for such withholding; it has occurred in other problem situations when appropriate solutions have been found in the course of action. Perception of the distance may be the relevant factor.

In the case of the other schemata, it is possible that there is minimal innervation of the appropriate muscles that is insufficient for action. This may be viewed as a gradual process during the preceding year, from full, overt action, to degrees of partial performance, to the minimal muscle innervation. An observation of Piaget's suggests how this process may occur. He described the behaviour observed at the age of five or six months, before the solution of barrier problems, as 'motor recognition'. Sometimes the partial performance, but not the whole sequence, of a behaviour pattern was evoked by an object that was related to that behaviour pattern. Piaget described the behaviour as 'outlining the movements'. One of the examples that he quotes is the following: he shook the hanging rattles which his son had often struck. The child looked at the rattles without letting go of the toy he held and outlined with the other hand the movement of striking (Ob. 107, O I). Piaget terms this behaviour 'recognitory assimilation'. Objects are recognized by the young infant in terms of the action he has learned to perform upon them and of the events thereby produced. In some instances this kind of behaviour was evoked when objects were not in their usual places. Hence the action is a means of registering an object as familiar, as an adult might in some situations comment, 'Oh it's only so and so'. The other feature was suddenness of the event.

It could be postulated that this 'outlining the movement' becomes more and more perfunctory until overt action disappears and only minimal muscle innervation occurs.

Evidence of minimal innervation of the muscles that would be used in action has been obtained when adults are asked to imagine that they are performing an action (Jacobson, 1930, 1932). Whether infants of eighteen months imagine actions, we do not know. Nevertheless a process from overt to 'implicit' action is often regarded as the way 'representation' of objects and events occurs in their absence and both Piaget (1953) and Berlyne (1965), from different theoretical positions, have argued that 'representation' is involved in the kind of problem solving under discussion. Berlyne (1965), for example, stated that he has adopted a widespread view when he says that 'covert representational processes, such as expectations, consist of sensorimotor processes that are prevented by inhibition from involving the musculature, except in an extremely attenuated way' (p. 346).

Piaget (1953, 1955) speaks of the 'representation' of objects that are not in the perceptual field and of spatial relations among objects other than as they are given in the perceptual field. He argues that the combination of schemata and 'representation' are interrelated, each being necessary to the other. He cites in support of this the behaviour of one of his children with a matchbox problem. The child had previously been presented with a chain in a matchbox that was partly open and she had learned how to remove the chain by hooking it out with her finger. When the opening in the matchbox was too small for her to do this, she at first tried to do so. At one point in her attempts, she suddenly opened her mouth. Piaget interprets this as evidence of the evocation of the 'making openings wider' schema, to be applied to a situation different from those in which it had previously been performed, with representation of the result.

Miller, Galanter and Pribram (1960) also spoke of people having a 'clear image of a desired outcome' (p. 38) when they execute a plan. The end-result towards which the sequence of actions is directed, in the stick problem, is grasping the object that is out of reach. For this the distance between the object and hand has to be reduced. If this changed spatial relation of hand and object is 'envisaged' or 'represented', this, together with perception of the stick, may evoke the 'move one object with another' schema. This may then in turn evoke the representation of the stick behind the object and the schema of placing objects near one another. If the sensorimotor schemata are evoked in a backward direction (the reverse order to that of the performance), we might suppose that the precise action would be selected: the requirement of decreasing the distance between object and hand leads to the selection of the correct direction of movement (towards the self) and this leads to selection of the appropriate placement of the stick (behind the object).

The next question then raised is what initiates the sequence of actions? The objection made earlier in this century to postulated 'representations' or 'expectancies' of the 'terminal goal' or 'desired end-result' was that these cannot themselves lead to action. Both Berlyne (1965) and Miller, Galanter and Pribram (1960), in a discussion of this referred to Guthrie's famous statement in this connection, to the effect that formulations of such cognitive processes leave the rat buried in thought; they do not produce action. The same argument is applied to human problem solving. This requires more than the representation of events that have been experienced and of those that may occur.

This is the core of the problem that Miller, Galanter and Pribram tackled: the relation of organized past experience to action. It was for this problem that they proposed the concept of 'plan'; they argued that this is as necessary to account for the behaviour of man as is the program for a computer. The relation of program to stored data does not imply that something acts upon itself. Hence the concept of an organizing process in man that operates upon stored experience does not imply a 'ghost in the machine' that operates upon itself. (See also Neisser, 1967, for a discussion of this point.)

The problem of the initiation of action introduces the question of motivation. Miller, Galanter and Pribram (1960) distinguished 'value', referring to the 'desired outcome' and 'intention' which they defined as the incompleted part of a plan that is already being executed. Action is initiated by an incongruity between 'the state of the organism and the state that is being tested for' (p. 26). In the present context the discrepancy between the necessary condition for grasping (object near hand) and the given greater distance is a state of incongruity. The 'test' to be satisfied, for termination of the sequence of actions, is that the object is within reach.

Berlyne (1960, 1963, 1965), in detailed discussions of the motivation of exploratory and epistemic behaviour, has introduced the notion of 'conflict', meaning a situation that evokes alternative responses or incompatible 'symbolic' responses when there is 'conceptual conflict'.

It should be noted that postulates concerning a central mediating process by which final 'desired outcomes' or the outcomes of the component actions are 'represented' does not necessarily imply 'anticipation' of a future event that has never before been observed to follow a certain action. Since it is argued that the coordinated solution sequence consists of sensorimotor schemata in the repertoire, the component actions have presumably been performed many times before in similar situations and the outcomes observed. What is possibly new is that children 'envisage' or 'represent' the outcome of the action that is evoked in attenuated form, instead of observing the outcome of the performed action.

The outcomes that are 'anticipated' in the stick problem are the altered spatial relations of objects in the perceptual field (stick and toy, and toy and hand). Piaget, who postulates the development of a general symbolic function during the second year, lists a number of other behaviours that require the postulation of the 'representation' of 'absent' objects (Piaget, 1951; Piaget and Inhelder, 1969b). One of these is finding a deeply hidden object. A second is making a response to a present object that has in the past been made to different objects, as when one object is used as if it were another; an example is pushing a stone along a wall and making the noise of a car. This may be regarded as the beginning of imaginative play. A third is the performance of actions that refer to events previously experienced; an instance of this is delayed imitation, for example, of some events of the previous day. A fourth kind of behaviour is looking outside the perceptual field for something that might be producing an event in it.

Apart from Piaget's (1951) observations on his children, we have few data on the occurrence of delayed imitation during the second year or upon the use of one object as if it were another. Evidence of imitation some time after the event has been observed is available for larger groups of older pre-school children from the results of the studies of Bandura and Walters and their associates on social learning (e.g. Bandura and Walters, 1963).

Imaginative play as a feature of the pre-school period is also well attested. There has been little study of children beginning to look for a causal agent outside the perceptual field when an event, not produced by the child, occurs within it. Piaget (1955) reports some instances in the second year. For example, while out of the child's sight, he moved an object to and fro or rocked a pram in which the child was sitting. The child looked round for a person (Obs. 157 and 159, CR). This behaviour implies that the child has finally distinguished between events that are produced by himself and by other agents.

The following thus appear to be 'represented' or recalled: static objects not in the perceptual field; the results of the movement of an object by the action of the child himself; and the actions of other people and the outcomes of them. Piaget (1951) and Piaget and Inhelder (1969a) regard the mental image as the vehicle of representation. Bruner (1964; Bruner et al., 1966) also regards the mental image as the principal means by which the pre-school child 'represents' that which he observes. The last question to be posed, then, concerns how these 'representational processes' develop.

It may be noted that the term 'representation' can give

rise to confusion and it might be best avoided. In the first place it is used in different senses by Bruner and Piaget. Piaget reserves it for the developments of the second year, described above. Bruner (1964) uses it throughout development to denote the means by which the child organizes his experience. The first eighteen months is a period of 'enactive representation', followed by one when 'ikonic representation' is added. Subsequently, from about the age of six or seven years an additional 'symbolic' mode of representation appears. Piaget denies that there is representation of action in early life, though he and Bruner appear to be using representation in different ways, rather than disagreeing over the sensorimotor character of the behaviour patterns of the first eighteen months. Moroever, Furth (1968) has pointed out that this term has three usages, one active, as when an individual's gestures 'represent' some event, and two passive, in broad and narrow senses, when one thing is being represented by something else. If representation is a word for the recall of past experience, new means of storage, in the form of mental imagery and words, can be described as such without need of a further term. If some term is required for the process of sequencing sensorimotor schemata that are minimally evoked, with a view to bringing about a different state of affairs, 'central mediating process' seems to be the most neutral one, in Hebb's (1966) sense, to indicate some other factor influencing behaviour than immediate sensory cues alone.

More important than terminology is how the child develops such mediating processes and new means of storage. The earlier discussion referred to the view that sensorimotor schemata became gradually so attenuated that they are evoked without action. These schemata, however, in fully overt form, are sequences of action and sensory feedback. We are now concerned with developments from the perception of objects and the observation of sequences of action performed by other people and the outcomes of them. Once the child has learned to dissociate his own actions from some of the events he perceives, an explanation in terms of the minimal evocation of the child's own actions that are associated with perceived objects and outcomes will not suffice. Piaget (1951) suggests that imagery develops from imitation: this, too, undergoes a process of change from overt action to minimal innervation (from external to internalized action in Piaget's terms). He appears, however (see Piaget and Inhelder, 1969a), to be extending the term 'imitation' beyond its ordinary usage, to include eye movements in visual perception. Perceiving an object is usually regarded as different from the matching of actions to a model, copying movements or sounds. This point apart, the existence of motor components in perception makes it possible to postulate that mental images of perceived events develop from actions in a similar way to sensorimotor sequences, involving movements of limbs. Berlyne (1965), too, has drawn attention to the possible role of receptor-adjusting responses, in the course of orienting reactions, drawing upon the views of Sechenov. This question probably cannot be considered apart from the development of perception in infancy. Gibson (1969) has recently reviewed the investigations and alternative theoretical formulations in this area.

Mental imagery, when it does develop, has been described as a new means for storing experience. A second new means of storage is language. Children usually begin to speak or comprehend a few words before the end of their first year. There are two developments at about the age of eighteen months – thus around the same time as the others that have been discussed.

One of the new developments is the combination in speech of two words – strictly of two morphemes, the smallest meaningful units of language. These combinations are new; they are not the result of imitation. The evidence for this is that they take a form that is not typical of adult speech. A small number of words is used frequently as the first member of the pair in a combination and a much larger class of words appear as second members (Braine, 1963; Brown and Fraser, 1964; Miller and Ervin, 1964). Examples are 'all-gone toy', 'all-gone mummy', 'up-cup', 'up-spoon' etc. Thus, near the time that children coordinate sensorimotor schemata, they combine verbal ones.

The second linguistic change is a rapid increase in vocabulary. McCarthy (1954) quoted a study by Smith, who found that vocabulary increases from an average of one to twenty-two words between the ages of ten and eighteen months; between one-and-a-half and two years the increase was from an average of twenty-two to 272 words. We might ask whether language plays any part in the other developments that have been discussed. Deaf children, observed by the writer, not taught language, solved problems of the insightful type, so clearly some language development is not necessary. These children also searched persistently for objects they had seen hidden under successive layers of covers. We might instead raise the question of whether the final development of that which Piaget (1955) terms the 'object concept' might account for or contribute to the rapid increase in vocabulary after the age of eighteen months.

Alternatively, or in addition, a learning set factor may be operative. In Harlow's (1949) original study of learning sets, monkeys were given series of hundreds of discrimination learning problems; eventually, after such a series, they solved the problems in the minimum possible number of trials. This is the second trial, since the chance-made choice on the first one gives the necessary information as to the correct object. If monkeys were presented with such problems every day, as the child is with 'word learning problems', a slow rate of acquisition would be followed by an increase in rate after the development of efficient learning sets. It would not be surprising if the cognitive changes discussed in this chapter led to or were accompanied by the capacity to form more efficient learning sets. This question cannot at present be directly answered. Studies of learning-set formation have been made of somewhat older children; it is unlikely that children of twelve to eighteen months could be induced to tackle long series of discrimination learning problems. We do, however, have some evidence on the final development of the object concept and on its concurrent development with problem solving of the type which has been interpreted as requiring prior sequencing of the actions.

The object concept

Piaget's techniques for the study of the object concept in younger children have already been described. Another technique he used for older infants is the 'invisible displacement' procedure. The investigator shows the child a small object, puts it in his own hand, then offers the child his fisted hand and lets him open it and take the object. The next time he does not offer the child his hand, but puts it under a cloth, lets the object fall silently, then removes his hand still closed and offers it to the child again, ensuring all through that the child is watching. If the child looks under the cloth after finding the hand empty, he is able to find an object after seeing the movements of its container, but not of the object itself. Piaget's variation on this procedure included placing his hand or the container under a succession of three covers. A different procedure was to hide an object under another and then to place three or four more covers in succession on top of that.

These procedures have been used by Lézine, Stambak and Casati and the writer, in the studies already referred to. The writer found a very close correspondence between retrieval of the object in these situations and solution of the stick or toy and bars problems in a group of severely subnormal children. Lézine, Stambak and Casati found a slightly lower correspondence, with the 'object concept' generally in advance of problem solving.

In order to determine whether children remember that a particular object has been hidden or that *an* object has been hidden, some procedure such as that used by Tinklepaugh (1928) with monkeys would be required. He hid a preferred food (a banana) under a cover and let the monkey find it, then, in later trials, substituted for this the less preferred food (lettuce), without the monkey seeing. That the monkey approached the correct cup with outstretched hand and took the banana, but did not touch the lettuce and searched further, or even screamed at the experimenters, indicates recall of the particular object that it saw hidden. Such recall in children might be inferred from continued searching or some form of protest if they found a block of wood.

Piaget's object concept, in fact, involves something more than the retrieval of a hidden object after a delay. The basic concept is that of identity: of the continued existence of the *same* object over time and through changes of position. Adults in Western society believe that the object that they find, after an interval of time and in the same place it was in when last perceived, is the same one that was there before. If the object is not there, the alternative explanations they would consider are that it is somewhere else, intact or in pieces, or that it has been destroyed. Unless they entertain ideas about immaterial agents, they assume that some person or an inanimate force has moved it. Even in societies where magical beliefs are common, no doubt people behave towards objects in their everyday lives in the same way; the exposure of children to beliefs probably comes later.

However, in some instances, it is not possible to know whether an object that is perceived is the same one that was previously perceived. This is so when there are many members of that class of object. An adult would have difficulty in saying whether the seagull that flew past his window yesterday – or even a few minutes ago – is the same one that is flying past it now – unless he has tracked it with his eyes the whole time. This is because of his knowledge of the fact that there are large numbers of seagulls in the area and that they tend to fly about in groups. But despite his knowledge of the fact that there are thousands of cups and saucers of the same colour, shape, etc., as those in his house, he would unhesitatingly say that these cups and saucers are the same ones that he bought – though he would be hard put to it to say which of them in the cupboard was the one he drank out of the previous evening, unless it has a special identity mark that distinguishes it from all the others.

Thus there seem to be several reasons why people believe that the object they now perceive is the one they perceived before. One is that it is in the same place; a second is that they have tracked its movements or those of its container with their eyes. A third is that, although neither of the above conditions operate, it has an identification mark that distinguishes it from other similar ones. A fourth, if the things are his own possessions, is that it is unlikely that anyone has exchanged them. The child, by the middle of his second year appears to have achieved the first three; it is unlikely that he has the fourth. Nor has he the necessary conceptual development to know when things might *not* be the same ones as before.

Concerning the first three, we need to know more about the cues for early recognition and its relation to the context of the child's actions. Some studies reported by Bower (1967) should be briefly mentioned, since they may be misinterpreted as indicating that the infant of seven to eight weeks has developed the object concept in Piaget's sense, though they are too complex to be described in detail here. Bower uses the term 'existence constancy' and takes as his starting point a distinction made by Michotte between perceptual existence constancy and a more conceptual kind which is qualitatively different and which corresponds to Piaget's object concept. Bower then asked whether the conceptual existence constancy, investigated by Piaget, develops out of the perceptual kind. An object was exposed to infants of forty-nine to fifty-five days and then made to disappear in various ways, for brief intervals, before reappearing. Various response measures were used in different experiments. One of the main findings was that the infants responded to the object in its absence, in certain conditions, for short time intervals and when the speed of disappearance was relatively slow. A second was a developmental change during the first year in respect of these two variables.

One of Piaget's (1955) main arguments concerning the development of the object concept is that it is closely related to the child's dissociation of the involvement of his actions upon objects in the occurrence of some of the events that he perceives. It has been pointed out earlier that objects disappear from the child's visual field and appear and reappear in it when he moves his head, as well as when objects are moved. One possibility that requires testing is thus that the infant learns to associate the movement of his head with the subsequent event of the appearance of an object.

A development such as that of the object concept is, of course, always the end-result of a long process of incremental change. Experiments such as Bower's begin to determine what some of these early changes are. Piaget (1955) has pointed out that the infant in this early period before he can grasp objects he sees, has much tactile and oral experience of objects, and responds to sounds from them, as well as having visual experience. In his view it is the integration of the experience of the object in different modalities that plays a part in the construction of the object. His interpretation of these coordinations is that separate visual, manual, oral and auditory schemata are developed and they are then coordinated by a process of reciprocal assimilation, when the infant grasps the objects that he sucks, looks at that which he hears, grasps the one he sees, and so on. Thereafter objects are assimilated into these coordinated schemata, not merely into the separate ones.

Moreover, more than a longer delayed reaction and the integration of successive events is required when the infant of eighteen months retrieves an object after tracking the movements of the container in which he saw it placed. This involves the 'understanding' of simple spatial relations between objects, as Piaget (1955) has pointed out.

It has been possible in this book to mention only a few of Piaget's numerous observations of his children. These contain many suggestions as to what may precede the development of the object concept. For instance, he reports the coordination of visual and tactile search only after grasping on sight has occurred. The manipulative behaviour patterns of repetitively turning an object round and round, while looking at the successive sides (observed also by the writer in older subnormal children), is a further, more complex instance of visual and tactile coordination.

When the child has learned that successive sensory events in different spatial contexts are of one object, he has yet a further problem to deal with. This is having to learn to distinguish between the successive reappearances of the one object and the successive reappearances of a number of similar objects. An oft-quoted observation of Piaget's is instructive. One of his children, at the age of two-and-a-half years, when out for a walk along the usual road, named a slug that she saw. Ten yards further on, she said, 'There's the slug again.' When asked whether it was not another one, she went back to the first one. Questions as to whether it was the same one or another one had no meaning. This child made the same statement about two red insects met successively, when she was over three years old (Piaget, 1951, Ob. 107).

This discussion brings us to the ability of people to construct classes of similar objects. The development of this is one of the topics considered in the next chapter. Before going on to this, it may be appropriate to summarize the differences between the various types of behaviour pattern that have been discussed up to this point and the inferences we may make about the infant's understanding of events that occur in his environment.

Summary and discussion

We began with undirected movements and reflex responses to stimulation from external objects. The former become directed first towards other parts of the body and towards external objects without producing a change in them as, for example, in visual following. These behaviour patterns were interpreted as simple feedback loops, of a regulatory kind, which led to the more complex behaviour of the visual control of hand movements and then to grasping visual objects. Five levels of behaviour were distinguished up to this point, mainly on the basis of the coordination of behaviour patterns of the previous level. The manipulative behaviour patterns which Piaget terms 'secondary circular reactions' were considered to fall into the fifth category; behaviour patterns which indirectly produce an event from objects, by a global movement of the whole body, were regarded as equivalent to the behaviour patterns of a lower level.

Piaget's (1953) classification of subsequent problem solving and manipulative behaviour patterns suggests that three more levels may be added. The sixth category consists of behaviour patterns that are the coordination of two of the previous level (secondary circular reactions). An example is removing a barrier in order to grasp an object that is behind it. The concurrent behaviour patterns are still termed 'secondary circular reactions' by Piaget, since the action is repeated in much the same form; their designation as derived secondary circular reactions indicates different features. The important feature, reported by Piaget, that merits further investigation is a pause between each of the repetitive actions taken up with observation of the result of that action. If the succession of actions when the infant shakes a rattle is too rapid for there to be time for regulatory feedback from each action to the next, the continuation of the sound would appear to be the condition for the continued repetition of the action. If there is a pause after each action until the event that is looked at or listened to ceases, the postulate of an interpolated observing action, between each manipulative action, is required. The solution of barrier problems may be a necessary prior development to this, since it may direct the infant's attention to the events that follow a specific action. This and the converse behaviour of using an adult's hand in order to produce again an event from an object suggest that the infant has learned the connection between the specific action upon the object and the ensuing event.

The pause between actions in manipulative behaviour may be the important development that leads to the acquisition of a new type of behaviour pattern that Piaget terms 'tertiary circular reactions'. These, together with the behaviour patterns by which solutions are found to problems of objects out of reach, form a seventh category. The manipulative behaviour patterns are a succession of actions that are a variation on a theme, or the repetition of a more precise action or both.

The basis for distinguishing them from those of the previous category is the linking of one action and the next, not merely by repetition, but by the modification of each successive action by the outcome of the preceding one. This may imply that the two outcomes are compared; this is more complex than pausing to look at the outcome of one action. Actions that relate two objects by the spatial relation of on, in or beside and the use of one to move another may be included in this category. When the appropriate support or string is pulled in these problems and when objects are placed in, beside or upon one another it is possible that the infant has learned about connections *between objects* that he sees. Similarly, his searching behaviour indicates that he has learned the relation of two objects when one hides the other from view.

Problem-solving behaviour which has been distinguished on the grounds of prior sequencing would form an eighth category, together with behaviour which suggests that the infant is taking account of the continued relation of masking and masked object when both are moved. The behaviour of looking outside the perceptual field for something that may be producing an event in it suggests that the child has learned that some of the events he observes are produced by himself and some not. If the concept of 'plan' is applied to behaviour in this last category, and also to that in earlier ones, a distinction has to be made in the way plans are formed before and after the age of eighteen months or so. Before this time the term refers to the sequencing in a certain order, on a subsequent occasion, of behaviour patterns that have already been performed in that order, the smoothed performance resulting from longer sequences of 'trial and error' action; after this it refers to the sequencing of component schemata before the performance of the actions.

A new kind of central event, a mediating process, has been inferred by some theorists in order to account for this prior sequencing and for the other developments such as the 'object concept'. It has been suggested, for example by Piaget (1953), that this takes the form of mental imagery. Whether or not this is so, the child does at some point store experience in the form of mental imagery – as he does also in the form of words. It is, thus, then possible to manipulate stored experience in this form when it is retrieved, in addition to manipulating objects themselves overtly. The implications of this for the kinds of actions that are performed upon objects will be explored in the next two chapters.

5 Learning Rules

The last chapter considered the development of unobservable internal events, the combination in new ways of existing sensorimotor schemata, which may loosely be termed 'thinking'. New forms of storage, mental images and words, may also be combined in new ways. Nevertheless, we are still concerned with the actions that the child performs upon objects – with the ways in which the internal processes are modified as the result of feedback from action. The reason for this is that higher levels of organization involve relations between objects and events or relations among the parts of a single object, rather than single, undifferentiated objects. These relations are of similarity in some feature such as colour or pitch, of differences in size, etc., of positions in space, distance, etc., of objects or parts of them within a whole, and the duration of temporal intervals.

When groups of objects are related by a common property we speak of 'classes'; such classes also may be related on the basis of a different feature which is common to the groups, as when classes of dogs, cats, etc., are combined into a class of mammals. Objects and events may be ordered in terms of differences, for example, of increasing size or duration of interval. Numbers may be applied to groups of objects and seriated elements and operations performed with the numbers alone. The various spatial relations among objects may be observed, reproduced, measured, as may temporal relations between events.

The next chapter will deal with the development of the child's capacity to classify, seriate, coordinate spatial and temporal relations and perform operations with numbers. This one will consider the developments that precede them, between one-and-a-half and six-and-a-half years. Thus, attention is directed to the actions that young children perform upon objects while taking account of the attributes and spatial relations: bringing together those that have common features but differ in other respects, relating objects by differences in size, ranking them in order, making regular spatial arrangements in lines and patterns, making patterns out of sounds. In enumerating, it is necessary to touch objects or point to them, while pronouncing the number names, co-ordinating each 'marking' action with the speaking of each number. The early development of enumeration may, therefore, be observed in the coordination of verbal and motor systems, with and without reference to objects, and in actions of putting objects into a one-to-one correspondence with others.

Rules and choice

'Rule' has become a fashionable term in the study of cognitive processes. Apart from reflex responses, choice is involved whenever an individual performs any one action and does not perform others that are possible in the situation. 'Choice' in this sense may be said to be involved when the infant bangs an object on a surface, instead of swinging it, rubbing it or carrying out any other action he has learned to perform with it. The conditions that lead to the selection of one kind of action (or response) of this sort have been extensively investigated among lower animals, with experimental variation of the conditions of outcome (or reinforcement), by Skinner (1938, 1953) and his followers.

Similarly, the selection of one object rather than another has been extensively investigated with child subjects in two-choice situations, response to one object being reinforced. When response is required to an attribute or spatial relation, choice is of some *feature*: the red one is 'correct', not the blue one, and not the one always on the left or right; or the left-hand one is correct, irrespective of colour, and the right-hand one is not. The number of possible choices is increased when the objects vary in more than one attribute. Consistently responding to the 'correct' one may perhaps be described as learning a rule. Rules vary in complexity. Two rules may be combined, as when the large red one, and not the small red one, nor the blue one of either size, is correct; or the rule may be of alternation of left and right positions.

In the study of the development of classification, seriation, number and the coordination of spatial and temporal relations, we are interested in how the child comes to handle rules that define relations among a group of objects. Consider the situation of choice when two objects are selected from a collection of ten or more, on the basis of a common property. If the objects vary in only one attribute such as colour, one, a red one, may be selected at random; in order to 'match' one of the same colour with it, selection of a red one, and not one of any other colour, has to be made. Recognition of similarity and discrimination of a difference are simultaneously involved.

To sort the whole collection on the basis of colour requires a continuation of such 'matching' actions, the continued application of the rule. When a collection varies in two or more attributes, sorting the objects into groups, on the basis of similar features, requires the consistent application of *one* rule and *not* of another, of colour for instance and not form or size, or form and not the other attributes. Thus, there is a choice of *rule* to be made. When we ask about the actions of children that take account of the attributes of objects, we have to ask how many attributes there are in a collection and how they are used by the child. A further question which will be considered in detail in chapter 6 is whether the child looks the objects over before sorting and works out a principle of classification or whether he develops it in the course of action.

Similarly, with actions that take account of spatial and temporal relations, we need to consider the question of choice in terms of the number of relations involved. Attention was drawn in chapter 1 to the difference between positioning an object in relation to others in one move, thereby taking account of all the relations at once and doing this by a succession of adjustments, dealing with the spatial relations one at a time.

It is possible here to discuss only a few of the questions that may be posed concerning these developments, partly through considerations of space and partly because some have not been tackled. Nevertheless, on some issues there is more relevant research than can be summarized in the short space of one chapter. Since the aim of this monograph is the illustration of a particular kind of analysis of behaviour, a few developments will be examined in detail and no attempt will be made to give a complete account of development in the period from one-and-a-half to six-and-a-half years. For this period the main problem is still that of the criteria which distinguish different forms of organized behaviour. One suggested criterion is the extent to which successive actions are linked, when the actions concerned unite objects on the basis of common properties, differences in size and spatial relations; this has to be related to that already mentioned, of the number of attributes and spatial relations involved. A further possible criterion is the kind of condition that terminates a sequence of such actions, whether this is an external or internal condition. This involves the associated question of an interpolated 'testing' action. The classification of behaviour along these lines raises questions concerning the 'holding' of the end-result to which the sequence of actions is directed and the holding of the rule being applied; these in turn raise questions on strategies for holding and for avoiding errors.

Direction towards an end-point

When the child sorts a collection of objects into groups, selects elements in order of size, copies a spatial pattern, and so forth, the activity has a definite end-point. The behaviour patterns that Piaget has identified as typical of children before they attain the prior sequencing and other developments just discussed are spinning and rolling an object, etc., and repetitively arranging and disarranging a few of a set of objects in or beside or upon others. These activities have no definite end-point; they could go on indefinitely. Let us, therefore, consider the behaviour of more advanced children when they handle material that does not require selection of a particular object from an array, or complex spatial placements. Examples of such material are a set of cubes and a box into which they may be placed, a stick and a set of rings that can be placed on it, a board with round holes in it and a set of round pegs that fit into them. Given this kind of material, children of eighteen months onwards place all the cubes in the box, all the pegs in the holes and all the rings on the stick, at least with collections of up to ten or twelve objects. This behaviour is so commonplace that it may be asked why it is singled out for discussion. It is worthy of notice only when contrasted with the earlier behaviour pattern of arranging and disarranging, of putting a few objects in or upon another, removing them, putting them back, removing them, and so on. The writer (Woodward, 1962b) has observed both kinds of behaviour in subnormal children with the kind of material described above. The putting and leaving behaviour was common among the children who solved the most advanced object concept problems, though a few displayed the in–out behaviour pattern. The latter was, however, more typical of children who did not solve the stick and advanced object concept problems.

The behaviour of putting and leaving all of a set of objects in a box or pegboard or on a stick may be distinguished on two counts from that of putting a few objects at a time in and out or on and off. One is that all the objects are used, compared with the use of only a few; the second is that *one* placing action with each is performed, when all are used, compared with several placing actions with each when only a few are used. A consequence of placing each object once is that the sequence of repetitive actions has a definite end-point, when all the objects are placed regularly elsewhere in holes, on sticks, in containers or upon one another. As already mentioned, none of the previous manipulative behaviour patterns described so far has had this feature. Putting in and out, dropping from different heights, spinning, rolling, etc., could go on endlessly. The conditions for the termination of the sequence of actions must be sought in completing events or conditions in the organism. There is thus a difference in the conditions for the termination of a repetitive sequence of actions. (That the child may repeat the whole sequence of putting and leaving each object is beside the point.) We thus appear to be dealing with the beginning of the continuation of a sequence of actions until a given end-point is reached.

What accounts for the change from in–out to putting-and-leaving behaviour during the second year? When a few objects have been placed in or on, the visual appearance of the changed spatial relations is the same in both cases. It could be argued that adults teach the latter behaviour to children and that they are able to do so when developments in language or imitation enable the child to understand what they say or imitate what they do. The writer has, however, observed many distractible, withdrawn and otherwise disturbed children, who do not respond to verbal instructions or do not look at or wait for a demonstration, but seize the material as soon as it is presented. The same change in behaviour is shown by these children, and also by deaf ones. Thus, adult instructions do not appear to account for the change in behaviour. It seems we must look for something else in the child. Is this a higher-order plan that includes a test phase for the termination of the sequence, the test being satisfied when all the objects have been used? Does this imply some 'anticipation' or 'image' of the outcome? This behaviour would be consistent with that of insightful problem solving, provided the analysis given of this is valid.

If a behavioural sequence of children of this age is governed by a plan of a kind that directs the actions towards an end-point, this is only so when the nature of the placement and the end-point are given in the form of the material. If there is a hole to put a peg in, box to put objects in, stick to put rings on, the end-point is given by the material – when all the objects are used and all the holes filled. When, on the other hand, objects are sorted by colour or form or when they are placed in a spatial arrangement such as a triangle, the arrangement is not given: there is more than one possible arrangement and hence selection.

Moreover, once young children have embarked on the course of repeating an action until a given end-point is reached, they cannot abandon it upon adult instructions to do so or when the conditions of a task demand it. This takes us on to consider a change in the conditions for the termination of a repetitive sequence: by external conditions, given by the material, or by a 'stop-rule' generated by the child.

Generation of stop-rules

Luria (1961) reported that children who start putting rings on a stick, when instructed to do so, cannot reverse the action when instructed to take them off, while the sequence of putting them on is in progress. Yet this is precisely what children do 'spontaneously' earlier, when they put a few on and then take them off. It would seem that once children transcend the earlier pattern of stopping a repetitive sequence before all the elements are used and go on to complete a 'task' with the whole set, the earlier behaviour cannot be reinstated!

Equipment more commonly used by Luria and his colleagues consists of a bulb that can be squeezed and a light that comes on and off as arranged by the experimenter. The task is to press the bulb while the light is on and not when it is off. Younger children, once they have started pressing the bulb, go on pressing when the light is off. Instructions to stop pressing do not achieve the required behaviour: the child responds by pressing harder or by giving up altogether. From about the age of three years, however, the children could be induced to press only when the light was on if the experimenter arranged that the child's action of pressing put the light out (Luria, 1961). Luria interpreted this in terms of feedback. A further factor is that the vigilance aspect of the task is reduced from two features to one. The child now has only to watch for the reappearance of the light and begin pressing; he does not also have to keep watching for the moment of its disappearance, since this now happens at a regular point, defined by his action of pressing.

The writer observed similar behaviour with different material. This was a set of cylindrical cups that varied in size and fitted into one another and formed a 'nest'. This has a high interest value for young children. The material was presented in nested form and the cups were taken out and placed separately on the table, the largest being left in front of the child. A set towards 'putting in' rather than building up was encouraged by standing the cups on their bases, with the open ends on top, and by instructing the child to put them back as they were. This problem was given to children of nineteen months to five years and to comparable subnormal children. In order to describe the 'going on and not stopping' behaviour, it is necessary first to give an account of the problems that arise through failure to select the cups by size and the strategies adopted by children to deal with them.

When children did not select the cups by size, they met the problem that one cup obstructed the entry of another. This has been called the 'obstruction situation' (see Figure 5).

A continuation of the same action, of putting cups in one another, in the vertical direction is prevented. One solution which some children adopt is to continue the vertical structure, without fulfilling the requirement of 'putting in', leaving the cup resting on the rim of the other if it will not go in. Another behaviour pattern that was present in young children under two years was to remove the cup that did not go in and to place it on others in the collection until one was found that it went into, whereupon it was left there.

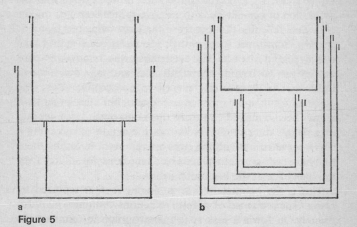

a   b
Figure 5

This, in fact, is another instance of a behavioural sequence that has a terminating end-point: that of getting an object into another. Again it would seem that the behaviour is directed towards a specific outcome.

A more advanced strategy to deal with the obstruction situation was shown by children of two-and-a-half or three years. This was to remove not only the obstructing cup, but also the one that obstructed it. Occasionally both were disposed of elsewhere, but more commonly children retained hold of the obstructed cup after removing it, while removing also the smaller obstructing cup and replacing it with the former. This strategy is more complex than previous ones; an object that is not visible is removed from a third object and replaced. The 'envisaged' or 'intended' end-result would appear to be to get the cup taken from the array into a particular cup, that on top of the main structure, and not merely into *any* one, as in the pattern of trying a cup on others until it goes into one.

When this strategy is applied consistently, success will be laboriously achieved in the long run because a cup larger than the one removed is placed in the nest, and in time it will be replaced by one larger, until the next in size eventually gets there. With practice children become very adept in the use of this strategy. Some get into difficulties, however, if they have a succession of smaller cups to remove rather than just one or two. The difficulties follow from their removing too many or too few. Sometimes they remove too many because they take out a handful at once, but even those who remove the cups one by one go beyond the right place and take out some of those that were correctly placed in consecutive sizes. The obstructed cup is then placed in the nest, but ones larger than it have been removed and from this point on children get into irresolvable difficulties. Sometimes the action of removing a cup is repeated until all the cups are removed, including those that have been correctly placed by a laborious procedure. They are then back at the beginning again.

This is the behaviour that is similar to that reported by Luria. The sequence of repetitive actions continues inappropriately. In Luria's task it is inappropriate in terms of the verbal instruction; in the nest of cups task it is inappropriate in terms of solving the problem.

Some of the children, however, adopted a procedure that enabled them to stop removing cups at the appropriate point, where all those smaller than the one that was obstructed had been taken out. Every time they had removed a cup, they placed the obstructed cup on top; if it did not go in, they removed another one. When it did go in, they stopped removing cups and this was, of course, the place where it was appropriate to stop. This may be interpreted as the insertion of a test phase and action after each of a repetitive sequence of actions, which is terminated when the conditions of the test are satisfied. The interpolated 'testing' action ensures that they stop at the appropriate point, before all the cups are removed. When children do remove all the cups, an external condition terminates the sequence – no more left to remove. When they try the obstructed cup on top each time after removing a cup, an internal condition terminates the sequence – a 'stop-rule' generated by the child.

So far we have distinguished two features of the behaviour of children who have achieved the developments described in the second part of the last chapter. One is continuing a sequence of repetitive actions until an end-point is reached, the end-point being given by the material. The other is terminating such a repetitive sequence when appropriate in terms of a different aim, before the end-point given by the material is reached. The second is considered to be of a higher level than the first by virtue of the insertion of a testing action, the generation of a stop-rule by the child in place of termination by an external condition.

On the basis of the present meagre evidence, this development may be placed about midway during the period from one-and-a-half to four-and-a-half years. Another development, on which we have also little information, may also occur around the same time. This is positioning a cube, in relation to another, in one move, rather than by successive readjustments.

To place a cylindrical beaker in another or a round peg in a round hole, presents no problems of positioning the sides of the objects with one another to be flush. Cubes do present such a problem. Young children who try to fit a 'nest' of cubes together have difficulty with such positioning. It is not unknown for them to discard a cube of the correct size that is not oriented correctly and to select another of the wrong size. Similarly 'towers' made by young children soon fall because the cubes are not placed full-square upon one another. The writer and Hunt (unpublished study) gave a box and four cubes to children. Very few of the children aged under three years positioned the cubes before putting them in the box, while nearly all those over three years did so. It might be expected, of course, that such prior positioning will be found to vary with the number of spatial relations involved.

The behaviour discussed so far in this chapter has either been with tasks that do not require selection (e.g. a round peg will go into any hole, a cube on any cube) or when selection is possible (e.g. in order of size) but the child does not adopt it. We turn now to selective actions that place two objects together on the basis of a common property or spatial relation.

Matching

'Matching' pairs of objects on the basis of similarity is the simplest action involving attributes. In order to select an object that is similar to another, from others that are different from it, prior developments in sensory discrimination are obviously necessary. There is evidence that some such discrimination has developed before the age of eighteen months, for differences in colour (Staples, 1932), simple forms (Ling, 1941; Welch 1939a) and some size differences (Welch, 1939b).

When children have made the advances in problem solving, language, the object concept, etc., during their second year, do they 'match' one object with another by, for example, selecting from a collection an object that is similar in colour or shape to another? A comparison of children who have and have not made these advances does not appear to have been made; such an attempt would encounter problems of method. A 'matching from sample' procedure, as used with lower animal subjects, would require children to sit and persist at the task long enough for a sufficient number of trials to be given for the relation of successes to the chance expectancy to be calculated. Welch (1939b) reported that children below the age of fourteen months were not motivated to tackle a two-choice discrimination problem, though children of seventeen months and over were highly motivated. On the other hand, the results of the spontaneous handling of a collection of varied objects are difficult to interpret. When children place together two objects that have a common property, this may be the result of chance. Since the pool from which the objects are drawn diminishes with each one taken, records are required of how many are left, after each move, of each colour and form, etc., if the chance expectancy is to be calculated. More-over, young children tend to scoop up several at once, whereas the matching from sample procedure ensures that only one choice is made at a time. The 'sample' is displayed apart from two other objects, one of which has a similar feature to the sample and the other not, choice of the former being rewarded. The child has thus first to learn what the game is about.

A compromise solution is to hold up a 'sample' and instruct the child to 'find one like this'. Similarly, when children are given a 'formboard' task, they show evidence of matching when they place a block on a hole of the same shape without first placing it on others. Evidence obtained by the writer from these last two sources, and that of Inhelder and Piaget (1964) on spontaneous handling, indicates that sporadic matching of pairs of objects is not absent in children of under two years, though how common it is is not known.

A development that might be expected from sporadic matching is consistent matching on every 'move' and sorting into groups a collection of objects that vary in only one attri-bute. Such sorting does not necessarily involve anything more than the successive matching of pairs of objects. It cannot be assumed that the sequence of actions is governed from the start by a 'plan' of sorting by the given attribute. Such sorting may be accomplished by selecting an object of the same colour as one that is separated from the array or by taking one, without choosing, from the array and placing it with one of the same colour. The advance made over the sporadic matching of pairs of objects, on the basis of a common property, would thus be that of such consistent matching on all moves, or most, followed by the correction of errors.

Preliminary data from a current investigation of the writer and colleagues indicate that children of three-and-a-half to four years can sort such a collection. A collection of objects that vary in two attributes presents a more complex problem. The way children of this age deal with such a collection indicates that they are in fact doing no more than successively matching pairs of objects when they successfully sort a collection that varies in only one attribute.

When children of three to five years are given a collection of objects that vary in two attributes and are instructed to sort them (in appropriate words), they may make spatial groupings rather than classificatory ones, for example, putting the base of a triangle along the edge of a square (Vygotsky, 1962); the result may be labelled, for instance, as a house (Inhelder and Piaget, 1964). When the collection consists of miniature real objects, Inhelder and Piaget (1964) report that children group them by their social experience rather than by logical criteria putting, for example, a baby with a cot and bottle rather than with people. Some children do, however, attempt to relate geometrical objects by a common property when they have a set that varies in two or more attributes, though they do not stick to the same criterion throughout. This keeps changing: they may, for example, place the elements in a line, taking first a yellow square and placing a yellow circle next to it, then a blue circle next to that, then a blue triangle. At some point a switch to form again is made (Inhelder and Piaget, 1964; Vygotsky, 1962). This would appear to be a matter of matching pairs of elements by one or another attribute. To place a blue circle next to a yellow triangle would not, of course, be matching at all.

When a collection of objects differs in only one attribute, being similar in other respects, the sorting task does not require the child to stick to the same criterion, for there is no choice of attribute to be made. When objects that vary in two attributes are sorted consistently by one criterion, *two* choices on every move are necessary: that of the criterial attribute (e.g. colour or form) that was the basis of the previous match and the particular instance within that attribute (e.g. a red one or a square one). For the repetition of the action of dual choice until a collection is sorted, a yet higher order plan has to be postulated. Thus, we may perhaps distinguish the successive levels of organized behaviour in the pre-school period by the number of choices involved in a sequence of actions that are repetitions of the same kind of action.

This analysis of sorting brings us to the distinction of a new level of organization: that when a sequence of actions involves a dual choice on every move. The instance discussed is sorting objects that vary in two attributes. Inhelder and Piaget (1964) report that children of five and six years succeed in sorting consistently by one criterion when three attributes are varied; the writer found that three-quarters of a five-year-old group did so when the elements varied in two attributes. During their fifth and sixth years children perform other tasks that may be analysed as sequences of dual-choice actions. These are the subject of discussion in the next section.

Pattern and order

When children sort a collection of objects by one attribute (e.g. colour) and not another possible one (e.g. size or form), they may be said to be selecting among the possible alternative rules – or at least consistently adhering to one rule when there is more than one that could be used. This requires selection of a particular kind of element from an array or selective placement with a class of elements. Such selection of a particular element from an array is involved when objects are taken in order of size. There is also selective placement when objects are placed in regular spatial arrangements, in patterns or in a certain order. Such behaviour may be described as rule-guided.

Some of the behaviour discussed so far in this chapter qualifies as rule-guided. It has been argued, however, that the rule is given in the material, when elements that vary in only one attribute are sorted, and the child has to make only a single matching choice on every move. When the objects vary in more than one way, choice of attribute for sorting has to be made, in addition to the matching choice: the rule is selected by the child.

A similar distinction may be made between the successive matching of pairs of objects and copying the order in which objects are placed next to one another in space. If a row of objects (e.g. of coloured cubes) is presented and the task is to place below each object a cube of the same colour, it is not necessary to choose the objects from the array in any particular order: any one may be chosen and placed below its opposite number. One matching choice is involved. This task may be converted into one of copying a spatial order if the child is given a rod and instructed to place beads on it in the order in which they occur in the other row. In this case it is necessary to select a particular colour from the array. In order to determine which particular element is required, the child has to refer to the model and note which one is next to the last one he copied. Two components are again involved.

The task of copying a spatial order may be presented in various ways. The simplest arrangement of a linear order is when the model and the rod for the copy are arranged parallel to each other and aligned end to end, so that each object on the copy is opposite its matching pair on the model. Children commonly achieve this during their fifth year. Subsequently, children reproduce the order correctly when their rod is displaced a little, so that the beads on the copy are no longer directly below their opposite numbers on the model, and concurrently they copy the order of elements arranged in a circle on to a rod. Later still they copy the row correctly if there are spaces between the elements and later still they can copy a linear order in the reverse direction, starting from the opposite end (Lovell, 1959; Piaget and Inhelder, 1956). In the displaced linear and circular conditions, it is less easy to keep track of the place of the last one that was copied.

When the elements are uniform (e.g. counters of the same

colour), children succeed in copying a linear arrangement with spaces between at about the same time that they succeed in reproducing a spatial order in the simplest condition: in a subnormal group the writer found that only five children managed the spatial order problem in this condition and did not make a one-to-one correspondence between two sets of spaced uniform elements. The rest achieved both. This correspondence again is not surprising: one involves preserving a qualitative relation between unspaced elements, the other a relation of distance between similar elements. Keeping one line parallel with the other means taking account of an additional spatial relation and further study may reveal that the achievement of this, in addition, is a slightly later development.

The copying of a square or rectangle with discrete objects such as counters, with spaces between them, in this way, has something in common with copying an outline square by drawing. In copying such figures the child has to chart his way through space on paper in a straight line and then at a certain point to take off in a direction at right angles to it in another straight line, as when placing counters. Again, taking account simultaneously of the spatial relations is involved. Copying a square, without 'ears' at the corners or curved lines, is an item for five year olds in intelligence tests (Terman and Merrill, 1937), the age at which Piaget and Inhelder (1956) found children copied a square accurately, as well as diagrams of two simple figures in certain relations.

A further example of the consistent application of a rule with two features, achieved during the fifth year, is in the task used by Luria (1961), described on page 134, of coordinating presses of a bulb with the appearance and disappearance of a light.

Children do, of course, increasingly make more correct choices or placements with the tasks described earlier, so we are discussing the end-result of a progressive change rather than an abrupt one. It is, however, the consistent performance on every move that is being stressed.

The difference in these consistent sequences of actions, compared with the earlier ones, appears to be that the actions are linked to one another by something more than a repetition of an action that matches two objects or places two in a spatial relation. What is added to this is making the match with the present pair on the same basis as that of the match of the previous pair. For example, sorting objects that vary in one attribute requires only the single choice of selecting or placing together two objects of the same colour or form or other feature. When they vary in two attributes, for example, colour and form, consistent sorting requires that the choice of attribute on each move should be the same as that on the previous one (form or colour); a second choice for the specific match (same colour or same form) has then to be made.

Kendler and Kendler (1962) made a similar point with regard to a change in the relative difficulty of different forms of reversal in a two-choice learning situation. They presented pairs of blocks at a time from among two larger ones, one black and one white, and two smaller ones of these colours. The correct block was, for example, the larger one. When this had been learned, two different kinds of reversal learning situations were presented: in one, the other size was correct, with colour still irrelevant; in the other form, colour was now relevant and size not, the correct one, for example, being the black one. The age trend was that the older children readily shifted when there was a change within the attribute (the other size was now correct) and the younger when there was a change from one attribute to the other (e.g. size to colour). The interpretation of Kendler and Kendler is that the older children, aided by verbal mediation, learned first the relevant attribute and then the specific feature within it, while the younger children learned only the specific features.

A point made by Inhelder and Piaget (1964) should be noted. Successful sorting by one criterion, when two or more attributes are involved, does not necessarily require looking over the elements, identifying the various attributes and selecting one. The result can be achieved by the chance selection of an attribute for the first match and then continuing subsequent matches within the same attribute. In this case the successive matching of pairs is still what is happening, though two choices, not one, are involved. This question of prior interrelating will be discussed later, as will that of whether seriation is a matter of interrelating all the elements or relating two at a time. It is sufficient to note for the moment the facts of the dual choice. If he does not select his rule at the beginning, the five and six year old must make his present match on the basis of his previous one, taking account of the criterion. To put it another way, the younger child is relating two objects by a common property, making one choice: the older child, who is making two choices at once, is relating three or four objects, which involves two relations. Two objects, for example, two squares of different colours, are related by the common property of being square; if a blue circle is then placed near a yellow circle, these two are related not only by the common property of circularity, but also by being placed together on the basis of form as in the previous match and not by colour. When this process continues, each successive action is linked to the previous one by the kind of match, not only by the fact of matching. Inhelder and Piaget (1964) term this 'successive assimilation'. The instruction or plan put into verbal form would be 'continue to match two objects in the same way' instead of 'continue to match two objects'. An additional test has to be inserted before the action of selecting or placing the element is made or, if errors are made and corrected, after it, in this case guiding the corrected placement.

With regard to the selection of elements in order of size, we should first note the difference in the behaviour of five-year-old children with a set of graded sticks that differ from one another by 0·8 centimetres ranging from 9 to 16 centimetres in length and 6·5 millimetres square at the base, and the nest of cups already described which differ from one another in diameter by 2·5 to 3·75 millimetres and in height by 2·5 millimetres. Children select a stick at random, compare it with another, discard it, take another, and so on. Once they have put two small ones together, they appear to be trying others until the difference between this and the second is perceptually equal to that between the first and second, and so on

(Piaget, 1952). They are thus applying the same rule to successive pairs of objects, as in sorting: they are equating the present two in accordance with the amount of the difference between the previous two. The piecemeal procedure is more evident in this case and supports this interpretation in the case of sorting when carried out by the same children.

In the writer's study, children who behaved like this with the sticks selected the cups by size or, when they had difficulty in perceptual discrimination, they occasionally took the next but one in size. The cups stood on an even base on the table, whereas the sticks lay on their sides not lined up on an even base nor even oriented the same way. When selecting a cup by size it was thus only necessary to look for the one that stuck up most, without having to do anything to make the comparison easier.

As noted already, the task of copying a spatial order also requires the selection of a particular element from the array on every move. Analysis of the spatial order problem reveals that the selection must be made with reference to the last action. The subject has to identify on the model the element that he has just found a match for, note the feature of the one *next* to it and select one like that from the array. The task thus has the same feature as that inferred in the problems of sorting and serializing sticks: this feature is referring to the previous action that related two objects when relating two more. In the spatial order task, the rule is 'next to'.

The concurrent change with regard to spatial patterns is to place a row of objects in a one-to-one correspondence with another row of spaced elements and to construct such rows or make columns of pairs of spaced elements. When tackling some number problems, for example, making two unequal groups equal in number, some five year olds make an arrangement of pairs of objects in columns and then copy this (Piaget, 1952). Whether the rule is one-for-one or two-for-two, reference to the previous action is involved, linking the sequence of actions. On the question of the number of spatial relations that are taken into account *before* an object is placed, we have little information.

It would thus seem that the new feature in the behavioural sequences performed by children from the fifth and sixth years onwards is that each action that relates two objects, on the basis of an attribute or spatial relation, is linked to the previous one that related two objects; previously the actions that related two objects were separate, not so linked. Any apparent links were given in the form of the material. It is thus no longer a matter of continuing the same kind of action, such as matching or aligning, but of referring to the way the previous pair was matched or spatially placed, this guiding the next match or spatial placement. A postulate concerning the process that controls a sequence of actions thus has to account for this linking of successive actions; in terms of a plan analysis, this is of a higher order plan that includes an additional TOTE.

A similar change, between four and five years, in the way children try to recognize blurred, complex pictures has been reported by Potter (in Bruner *et al.*, 1966), who also refers to an absence in the three and four year olds of an 'active directed process'. The children produced a string of unrelated guesses for different parts of the picture and they were not bothered if successive hypotheses referring to different parts of the picture were incompatible. The older children, in contrast, made some attempt to relate successive guesses. This is similar to the difference between changing the criterion while sorting and sorting consistently by it, in fact to performing a sequence of unrelated, single-choice matching actions, compared with performing related, dual-choice ones.

A further point that Potter mentioned was that younger children were very readily guided by their own personal experience, making a guess on the basis of a personal association. Piaget (1951) and Lunzer (1964) discussed the implications of the verbal inferences of young children for the way they categorize – or rather fail to do so logically – by interpreting events inappropriately in terms of their own particular experience rather than by objective relations. An illustrative example quoted by Lunzer (1964), from Susan Isaacs, concerning a four year old, is instructive. Two children were looking at a picture of a ship and its lifeboats which one of them named. The other denied this, adding 'Lifeboats don't be on the side of a ship, they are on the cliff in a long shed.'

Extraction and retention of the rule

We have considered the performance of a sequence of actions in accordance with a rule that is selected; the other relevant aspect is the extraction of a rule, of identifying the recurrent regularities in a set of objects or events. The older method of examining this was in a two-choice discrimination learning situation, with procedures developed originally for lower animal subjects. Food was placed under one object or in a well under a card with a symbol on it and not under the other object or card. When the procedure was used for young children a sweet or small toy replaced the food reward; when a common response to one object (or picture of one) was established, variations with a common feature were introduced, in order to study 'concept formation'. For example, in the study of Long (1940), a variety of round objects were used after children had learned to respond to a circle and not to other shapes.

A similar procedure has been used for adults. The classic study of adult concept formation is that of Hull (1920). Sets of Chinese characters that had a small common feature were used and a nonsense syllable was paired with each set. When the subject had learned the nonsense syllables for a member of each set, he was then presented with other instances and instructed to 'guess' their names. Bruner, Goodnow and Austin (1956) argued that such a procedure which presents the instances successively does not permit adults to use their advanced processing systems, because they are not allowed to see the whole set of instances in one array. They did this, presenting on a board an array of ninety-one cards; these varied in four attributes in three ways (three colours, one, two or three figures, three forms and one, two or three borders), with all possible combinations given. The experimenter chose a concept (e.g. all cards with green circles) and the subjects' task was to discover it in the smallest number of moves. The subjects designated one card and were informed whether or not it was an instance of the concept; when they judged they had attained the concept, they were to state it. By utilizing the information, positive or negative, the subjects could make inferences concerning which attributes were relevant or irrelevant to the concept, by comparing this card with others that were and were not instances. They could thus select every card except the first with a view to gathering information that would permit them to draw another inference. For example, if the first card was positive and had three green circles and one border, they could select a card with one attribute varied, e.g. one with two green circles and one border. If this card were found to be an instance of the concept, clearly number was not a relevant feature; a next logical selection would be a card with colour, or the number of borders or form varied.

Analysis was made in terms of strategies of this kind, a comparison being made of possible 'ideal' strategies that could be adopted with those used by the subjects. The study of rule extraction, hypothesis formation and the use of strategies in adults has been extensive in the last twenty years.

Study of the two-choice learning situation has, however, led to a finding which is of importance for conceptual development; equally it is one in which strategies adopted by subjects may be examined.

The finding is that which Harlow (1949) has termed 'learning set'. This arose from the procedure of presenting subjects (monkeys in the first instance) with as many as a hundred problems with different pairs of stimuli, instead of merely one problem for a number of trials. With practice with a series of problems, learning becomes gradually more efficient with that particular kind of problem, until it is solved in the minimum number of trials possible. In the two-choice learning situation, this is two trials, since the first gives the necessary information: whether the first chance selection is correct or incorrect, it indicates under which object or symbol the 'reward' is to be found, once the subject has 'got the hang of the game'.

In the original studies of Harlow and in later studies of

pre-school children (see Reese, 1963, for a review) two-choice learning situations of varying complexity have been used. It is likely, however, that learning sets are formed also in relation to more complex problems than any of these. The chess-master who goes from game to game, quickly making a move at each table, has probably a large stock of high level learning sets in relation to chess problems. Using another language, the individual, throughout development and adult life, goes on adding to his store of 'subroutines'.

Harlow (1950) also initiated the study of the strategies used by subjects in two-choice learning situations, by making an analysis of the kinds of errors made by monkeys with these kinds of problems. Possible relevant ones are position of the object (left or right) and some feature of the object or symbol, or combination of features. Harlow's analysis was in terms of stimulus perseveration and differential cue errors, response shift and position habit errors. Levine (1959) followed this up with an analysis of sequences of choices that followed a correct or incorrect choice. Consistent patterns of response followed a 'win' or a 'lose' on one side or the other and a win or lose with one of the objects.

These patterns have been termed 'strategies'. A lose-object change-object strategy, for instance, is a shift to the other object next time, following a choice of the incorrect object.

The analysis of the patterns of errors in two-choice learning situations has revealed differences between monkeys and children, and between children of different ages. Reese (1963), who reviewed the literature, reported a study by himself and Levinson in which pre-school children were found to differ from eleven year olds. The strategies of the latter were logically related, whereas the win and lose strategies of the younger children were inconsistent. Alternative hypotheses to account for this included an attentional deficit, the reaction of young children to failure and limited verbal mediation.

Bruner *et al.* (1966) have extended their kind of strategy approach to the study of children. In one investigation, for example, Olson (1966) presented children with the task of finding out which of two or three patterns was 'correct'. They could find out by pressing bulbs on a board. The patterns were displayed above the board, with spots representing bulbs, and the board was so arranged that bulbs which duplicated the pattern lit up when pressed, while others did not. Pressing the latter would thus provide no useful information. The patterns always had a common line. For example, one pair of patterns was an upright T and the other was the cross-bar of the T in the same position. A bulb in the top line would thus light up when pressed, but would not give any information as to which pattern was correct. Any bulb down the vertical line of the T would, however, be informative. This problem could be solved with one press; others with different patterns and more than two required a minimum of more moves, together with the 'holding' of the information from the first press.

Children in the group with a mean age of forty-six months, while not random pressers, did not confine themselves to bulbs on the pattern. They proceeded in an orderly manner across the board, apparently looking for which bulbs lit up, without using the patterns above as a guide. A 'striking change' is reported of the five-year-old group. They confined themselves to the bulbs that corresponded to the patterns (thus referring to the patterns above the board), though they worked through the whole pattern pressing both redundant and informative bulbs.

The behaviour of five year olds in rule extraction is thus systematic, as it is in rule application, but the capacity to seek information in a way that permits an inference to be drawn is limited.

When a sequence of actions is carried out in accordance with a rule, it has to be retained while the actions are performed, whether it is abstracted by the child from the elements or whether it is given in the form of a verbal instruction. This raises the question of what accounts for the retention of the rule throughout the sequence of actions. The relation of the improvement of some aspect of short-term memory might usefully be investigated in this context. A further point on this question is that it may be a different matter to retain a rule (verbal or otherwise) while carrying out a sequence of actions in accordance with it, from retaining a verbal message of the same length for a similar length of time, while doing nothing or while performing other actions.

In terms of the kind of analysis that has been made of the 'five-year behavioural change', there are two aspects which involve memory. One is retaining the rule; the other is retaining the specific feature of the object to be matched. In the spatial order problem, for instance, the general rule of copying the order of the elements on the model has to be remembered and so has the colour (or other feature) of each element while its opposite number is being selected from the array. This leads to questions about changes in the factors that facilitate remembering and changes in the strategies that children adopt in order to remember.

The latter one is a virtually unexplored field. Reference was made earlier to the studies reported by Bruner (1968) concerning the strategies of action used by infants to keep track of what they set out to do, while performing an intermediate action. Belmont and Butterfield (1969), who reviewed the recent studies of short-term memory in children, reported a study on the strategies used by children when they attempt to remember the spatial position of an element.

Concerning strategies for remembering in the kinds of problem that children solve in their fifth year, Piaget and Inhelder (1956) report that children who succeed with the spatial order problem frequently touch the 'next' element on the model or speak its colour name. The writer and Hunt found that both touching the model and naming the colour significantly differentiated between children who did and did not succeed with this problem. The rule of verbal rehearsal in the recall of a succession of different items has also been demonstrated in six year olds, for example, by Flavell, Beach and Chinsky (1966).

Piaget and Inhelder (1956) attribute considerable theoretical importance to such motor components in the development of spatial concepts, though language has a lesser place in their scheme. The child does, however, have to turn away from the model in order to select an element from the array and he has to remember what colour to select. Children who do not speak the colour name, silently or aloud, may use a memory image. Evidence of the role of imagery in the problem solving of pre-school children has been provided by both the Harvard (Bruner *et al.*, 1966) and the Genevan (Piaget and Inhelder, 1969a) groups.

The role of naming in the learning of pre-school children has been much investigated in recent years (see Cantor, 1965, for a review) and a current concept, put forward to account for improvements and changes in children's learning during their fifth and sixth years, is that of 'verbal mediation'. The converse of using language in order to retain a rule that is given verbally or is extracted by the subject from a set of instances is to be able to state verbally the basis of correct choices. In older studies of simple two-choice learning situations (e.g. Heidbreder, 1928; Hunter and Bartlett, 1948), it was found that children from the age of five years more often named the principle that they learned, in double-sign (e.g. near and coloured) and double alternation (twice on the right and twice on the left) problems. Kuenne (1946) similarly found that it was also at about this age that children could state the basis of their learning in transposition problems. It was this study that initiated the current interest in verbal mediation. The use of language by pre-school children is, however, not always precise, particularly in the use of words that refer to relations between the attributes and so forth of objects. Donaldson and Balfour (1968), for instance, found that children of three-and-a-half to four years appeared to use the words 'more' and 'less' as synonyms.

This question of verbal mediation has too many ramifications and unresolved issues for it to be discussed in detail here. Discussions and reviews may be found in Kendler and Kendler (1959, 1962 and 1963) and in Reese (1962). An alternative formulation has been made by Flavell and his associates in terms of a 'production deficiency', rather than deficiency in verbal mediation earlier in the pre-school period (Flavell,

Beach and Chinsky, 1966). This is to the effect that the child has the necessary cognitive skills, but is unable to utilize them when tackling problems. These workers suggested, moreover, that the cognitive skills that are not produced may be non-verbal as well as verbal (Corsini, Pick and Flavell, 1968), and even the main proponents of a verbal mediation hypothesis have stated that the mediation is not necessarily verbal (Kendler and Kendler, 1967).

Bem (1970), on the other hand, used both the mediation and production concepts when she suggested a three-stage process from comprehension, to production, to mediation. Lack of comprehension is defined as failure to achieve an adequate representation of the end-result of the problem. She found that children who could not perform a task upon a verbal instruction could do so after they had seen the end-result. The child was given a block to hold and presented with another of a different colour; the task was to 'make it so that the red block is on top of the blue one'. Confirming a previous result of Huttenlocher and Strauss, Bem found that children of three-and-a-half to four-and-a-half years could succeed when they held the red block but not when they held the blue one. When shown the correct arrangement before they started, they were able to solve the problem in the second condition and to do so in new similar problems without being shown the end-result.

This discussion of the period from one-and-a-half to six-and-a-half years began by referring to the possibility that children begin, in their second year, to envisage the end-result of a sequence of actions before they perform them. A further suggestion, in the light of Bem's study, may be made to the effect that there is a development in this period of ability to envisage the end-result of increasingly complex sequences of actions. The end-result of placing cups in other cups, rings on a stick, a set of six pegs in holes in a board, without reference to order, if the elements vary, is merely a matter of placing a collection of objects somewhere else. The end-result of copying a spatial order, sorting objects by one criterion, placing objects in spatial patterns, etc., involves interrelations among the objects. Whether five- and six-year-old children envisage complex end-results of this kind when a model is not given (e.g. in sorting or making spatial patterns) may be doubted if the interpretation is correct that they are proceeding step-by-step, matching two objects or positions on the basis of the relations of the previous match.

This question will be taken up again when the limitations of the advances made in the fifth and sixth years are discussed. Before going on to this, there is a final question to be considered in relation to this advance. This concerns the possible role of the inhibition of impulsive action as a factor in the performance of dual-choice sequences. The selection of a particular object from an array requires withholding the action of taking any other one. This, in fact, means inhibiting a system of selection on the basis of proximity, in favour of a system of selection by the principle. Children's hands may be observed hovering over one element before passing on to the correct one. S. H. White (1965) also reported a qualitative observation of this kind, along with his quantitative findings that provide evidence for his interpretation of the behavioural changes that begin at the age of about five years. This interpretation is that the first-learned, now inappropriate response, competes with a second-learned, correct one, the former being minimally elicited and inhibited in favour of the latter. White's evidence is based upon his results from simple two-choice situations. For example, when response A had been learned to a stimulus, response B was then required to the same stimulus. Performances of the now incorrect response A were quicker than performances of response B. The interpretation of the difference in the latency of the response was that the stronger response was first minimally elicited and then inhibited. Luria (1961) made the same point, concerning the inhibition of inappropriate action, in connection with the coordination of actions with an external event, in the bulb-pressing task referred to on page 134. Children of four and a half years or so press the bulb only when the light is on, without the previous aids which three year olds require. They thus inhibit the action of pressing the bulb continuously.

S. H. White (1965) reviewed the behavioural changes that occur from the ages of five to seven years, including some of those discussed here, along with others. His general interpretation of them is of the inhibition of the 'impulsive', most readily available action, though he suggested two possible interpretations. One is that any number of competing responses are 'temporally stacked': the first-learned, or most reinforced, response is most readily available, with the shortest latency, and the others are arranged along a 'time zone' in different degrees of availability.

The other possibility that White considers is that there are only two 'zones', one of automation and one of decision. In the former system are 'over-learned' responses with short latencies. In the event of novelty or some other feature, the subject inhibits the response in the automated system and switches to the decision system for selecting among the remaining alternative responses. Such selection is achieved by reflective operations, which can override the temporal priorities among the responses.

In his theoretical discussion, White does not distinguish between the earlier changes and those that occur from seven years onwards, on the basis of differences in complexity. The writer, following Piaget and Bruner, makes such a distinction. Hence a discussion of White's views will be deferred until these other changes have been described.

So far the advances made by children of five and six years have been considered. We turn now to examine their limitations when compared with the further advances made subsequently.

6 Thinking Ahead

We have just considered the actions of children that take account of the attributes and spatial relations of objects. The reason given for doing this was to examine the early development of systems that enable the individual to discover relations between events and the principles that govern them or to understand an exposition of them. This chapter deals with these systems.

Such discovery and understanding require the classification of phenomena, the application of number and the measurement of continua; they also require the individual to make logical inferences about relations between sequential events. Behavioural sequences are organized at higher levels to the extent that they take a form such that the outcomes of the actions may be compared and logically related. A scientific experiment is an example of a high level of organized behaviour, when the aim is to devise a procedure that will give an unambiguous answer to the question that is posed. A sequence of actions is thereby linked or coordinated by prior consideration of the outcome. Our main concern is thus with the development of the capacity to anticipate the possible outcomes of actions before they are performed and to organize the sequence of actions to produce outcomes that may be compared in a way that will test a hypothesis concerning causal relations between events.

This involves the capacity to make logical inferences between observed concurrences of events. The final form of organized behaviour which we shall examine is thus that which enables the individual to handle interrelations within three spatial dimensions, to apply complex measuring instruments, to perform mathematical operations and to examine interrelations between several comparisons and draw logical conclusions from them.

We shall first consider, however, a lower level of organized behaviour, which is a halfway house to the final one, though it is also an advance on anything discussed so far. The individual can handle interrelations within two dimensions, apply elementary numerical operations and begin to measure, and relate two comparisons, judgements and hypotheses.

These changes occur commonly from the seventh year onwards. Different interpretations have been put forward concerning them. Piaget and Inhelder advance the concept of 'operation', which they define as an integrated system of internalized actions that are reversible. They distinguish a lower order kind (concrete) from a higher order kind (formal). Bruner (1964, and in Bruner *et al.*, 1966) conceives of the changes in terms of a new means for coding and re-ordering experience by a new use of language.

Relating two rules

The lower order systems will be examined first. Although there are variations in the age at which children begin to make the transition towards different kinds of behaviour and central processing and achieve them consistently, results from various sources (e.g. Bruner *et al.*, 1966; Elkind, 1961; Lovell, Mitchell and Everett, 1962; Piaget and Inhelder, 1969b) suggest that, in technological cultures at least, it is between the ages of six and a half and eight years that about 70 per cent of children in the age group commonly achieve a new level for various developments. Consequently, for the sake of brevity, this will be referred to as the 'seven-year change', though this usage should not be taken to imply that no child begins to reach it consistently before this age, nor that none do after it. Indeed, subnormal children are several years older before they begin to achieve it (Lovell and Slater, 1960; Lovell, Healey and Rowland, 1962) and some subnormal adults do not achieve it at all (Woodward, 1961, 1962a). Furthermore, it should be borne in mind that we are not discussing a change that occurs for all areas in the course of a few weeks. Children begin to behave and think in a new way in one area and gradually extend this to others.

Our first task is to contrast the behaviour described in the last chapter with that from which a new level of organization is inferred.

When children are confronted with tasks of sorting, putting in order of size, copying spatial orders and patterns, in the manner described in the last chapter, it is not a necessary inference from the behaviour that they consider all the inter-relations of the attributes of the elements before acting – let alone their relation with other members of the classes not present in the array – nor that they consider the spatial inter-relations among the objects and relate these to an abstracted spatial framework defined by horizontal and vertical axes. The alternative interpretation, suggested by Piaget and Inhelder (e.g. 1969b; Inhelder and Piaget, 1964), which has already been mentioned, is that the child proceeds retroactively, relating the objects two at a time in a piecemeal fashion, which Piaget and Inhelder term 'successive assimilation'. Clearly, different problems from those described earlier have to be presented to children of five and six years and to older ones who may be expected to show more advanced processes.

Behaviour will be discussed in two situations. One is when a change in a rule or a hypothesis is required in the face of changed circumstances or new evidence. The second is when it is necessary to take account simultaneously of two rules or relations among groups of objects. This will lead to a discussion of precision and the adoption of systematic approaches.

New evidence and change of rule

We saw in the last chapter that children of the age of five and six years can sort objects consistently by one criterion, in con-trast to their earlier behaviour of changing the basis of the classification. When required to make such a change, however, in view of a new situation, they are unable to abandon the criterion they have used. Inhelder and Piaget (1964) report a study in which children were instructed to sort a set of elements into two classes into two boxes; when they had done this, new elements were successively added that required each time a change of the criterion of the classification for the whole set or at least for the subdivisions in it. For example, the original set included two forms of the same colour, size and material. The first additional elements introduced a difference in form and colour; the second ones were larger than any so far sorted and of two other forms and colour. The third ones were of still yet new forms and of different material from all the rest – corrugated, not in smooth card as were the others. Children of five and six years, unlike those younger, attempted in a trial and error manner to take the new attributes of the additional elements into account, but they did so within the framework of their first classification by attempting to contain the additional elements by subdividing the first groups, but not achieving a consistent subdivision. The change from flexibility in the criterion used in the pre-school years, to successful adherence to the same criterion, has been achieved at the expense of inflexibility when a new situation demands change. We have already met a similar situation: children of two years who have made the advance from in–out behaviour to putting and leaving, using all the objects, cannot abandon the repetitive sequence once they have started. In the present instance, however, the action that is repeated is more complex, involving a selective, dual-choice action. By the age of seven or eight years children change the criterion of the main classification or of the first subdivision when necessary and make different subdivisions without contradictions.

A further example of the way in which a previous action with an object 'fixes' the actions with subsequent ones is revealed in another study reported by Inhelder and Piaget, on the handling of complementary classes by children of five and six years (for example, flowers that are not tulips are the complementary class to tulips in the class of flowers). Children were given a set of pictures of flowers consisting of one kind of flower of different colours, for example, tulips, and four other kinds of flowers, or pictures of apples and four different kinds of fruit. They were required to sort these into two groups. When they had done this, additional flowers or fruit of different kinds were brought in. Some six year olds who made groups of apples and of 'other fruit' or of tulips and 'other flowers' could not add a different kind of fruit or flower to the 'other kind' group unless there was already a representative of that kind in the box. For example, a child aged six years four months, put the primulas in one box, because 'they are all the same thing', and put the rest in box two. He stated that the contents could be described as 'primulas' and 'a mixture', respectively, but when asked where snowdrops would go, he replied that a third box would be needed, 'because it's another flower'. He was specifically asked whether it would be correct to place it in box two, containing 'the mixture', and he denied this on the grounds that there was none like it inside. When asked a similar question about a rose, he allowed it to go into box two, because there were already some like it inside.

This supports the interpretation that these children, in sorting tasks, are linking the present matching action with a previous one: when there is no representative of a kind of flower present, there is no previous matching action for such a retrospective link to be made.

A different illustration of 'fixedness' is given by the study of Bruner and Kenney (1966). The task consisted of arranging nine glass beakers that differed in height and diameter into a 3×3 matrix. The beakers were shown arranged in three columns and three rows, with diameter increasing across the rows and height increasing up the columns. The shortest, thinnest glass was in the bottom left-hand corner, and the tallest, fattest one was in the top right-hand corner.

One of the two main tasks was to place the glasses back in this matrix when they had been disarranged; the other was to do so with the shortest, thinnest glass in a different place, the bottom right-hand corner, when they were again disarranged. In the first task the glasses had to be replaced in the positions in which they had been seen; in the second the form of the matrix had to be preserved, but each individual glass had to be in a different place.

From the age of five years the matrix was correctly copied in the first condition, but none of the five year olds succeeded with the second task and only about 20 per cent of the six-year age group did so. There was a sharp increase in successful performance and in the number of glasses correctly placed from the six-year-old to the seven-year-old groups. Inquiry revealed that the younger children were trying to remember where the glasses had been. This would, of course, serve well for the first task, but be useless for the second. The interpretation of Bruner and Kenney was that the younger children relied on a memory image of the arrangement that they saw, while the older used a more advanced linguistic coding system. The child who said 'It gets fatter going one way and taller going the other' (Bruner and Kenney, 1966, p. 165) provides an excellent illustration of this.

Coordinating two relations

Further evidence of the limitations of the advances made by five- and six-year-old children is seen when they use their capacity to copy spatial patterns in order to solve certain number problems. For example, if given a task devised by Piaget (1952), of giving 'your friend as many sweets' as are in a row of spaced elements on the table, they place another set of objects in a row below in a one-to-one correspondence with the other set in order to solve this problem. In another of Piaget's number problems the child is presented with two unequal groups of counters (e.g. six and sixteen) and is instructed to make them equal in number. Some children succeed in doing this by placing the smaller group into a regular arrangement, such as three pairs, in a column, and then making a similar pattern with six of the larger group; they then put a pair of objects alternately to each side. Another instance of lack of flexibility is seen when the total number of counters is not divisible by four. They place the last pair to one side, see that this makes that pattern longer than the other, switch the pair to the other side and see that that is then the longer. They may move this last pair from side to side several times before hitting on the solution of splitting the pair and putting one to each side. The rule is, thus, still 'repeat the same action' although the action itself is more complex than before four and a half or five years.

In addition to the above behaviour, the writer has observed children and subnormal adults who count the objects in both groups. They move some from the larger to the smaller group and count again and so on until they arrive at the same number name for each group. One subnormal adult was observed to move only one over at a time starting with six and sixteen, counting each time. When he had ten in one group and twelve in the other and had moved one more over, he was asked whether they had the same number now; he replied 'I'll have to count to find out.' The limited understanding of number that is given by being able to count is obvious.

Moreover, the reliance of these children on the similarity of the patterns prevents an understanding of number as independent of the spatial arrangement of the elements. This is most clearly brought out by the best known of the Genevan experiments, those on the conservations. If children solve the second of the above two problems by making two equal groups with similar patterns, such as columns of pairs of objects, the pattern in one group may be disarranged, so that the objects are scattered irregularly over a larger area than that covered by those in the other group. Some children then deny the numerical equivalence of the two groups, stating that there are more in the group that covers the larger area. Similarly, with the first problem, if one row is extended so that the elements are no longer opposite, five- and six-year-old children commonly state that there are more in one row than in the other. They appear to be guided by the difference in the areas covered or in the lengths of the two rows, ignoring the differences in the distances between the objects in the two groups or rows. Repeated evidence of the correspondence, when the patterns are made similar again, does not change their view when one pattern is disarranged – though doubt may be aroused in children who are moving towards 'conserving' the invariance of quantities through changes of state.

In another variation (Piaget, 1952), liquids are poured into two glasses of the same shape (A_1 and A_2) to the same level and the contents of one (A_2) are poured into another of a different diameter (B) and questions are asked about the equivalence of the quantities in glasses A_1 and B, reasons for the answer being requested. The child who maintains that there is more in the taller, thinner glass because the water level is higher is again comparing only one of the two relevant aspects.

Piaget, Inhelder and Szeminska (1960) report studies of the conservation of length and area. The procedure is similar. Two equal sticks are placed parallel, with the end-points coinciding, so that the child can see the perceptual equivalence. One is then displaced to the right, so that the end-points no longer coincide. Again, children who do not affirm the equivalence say that one is longer; they do so also when two sticks that have been seen to be perceptually equal are placed at right angles and when one is left straight and the other is broken up and made into a zigzag form. Similarly, if two sheets of paper of the same dimensions, representing 'fields', have 'houses' all of the same size and shape placed on them one by one, close together in one field and scattered in the other, young children state that the space left uncovered in the field with scattered houses is less than that in the other.

In the study of the conservation of weight, two balls of modelling clay are shown on scales to be of equal weight. One is then made into a different shape or broken up into smaller pieces and the children are asked whether the two pieces or groups still weigh the same or whether one is heavier than the other. If the child claims that one is now heavier, he may be given evidence of the equivalence if the two pieces or the large one and the set of small pieces are again weighed. Piaget and Inhelder (1969b) report that the conservation of weight is two years later in developing than the conservation of substance, while shorter time lags exist between the other conservations described above. They also found that the conservation of 'displaced volume', when a solid object or something that dissolves is placed in liquid, develops yet another two years later. Lovell and Ogilvie (1960, 1961a and 1961b) confirmed this sequence in the conservation of substance, weight and volume.

These studies of 'conservation' and 'non-conservation' have been replicated elsewhere in numerous investigations outside Geneva – though rarely as comprehensively. While there may be controversy as to the process of change to conservation, the facts of the behaviour are substantiated.

The attainment, too, affects judgements of quantity when equivalence has *not* been previously demonstrated. Clough (personal communication) presented children with pairs of different glasses containing water, as illustrated in Figure 6.

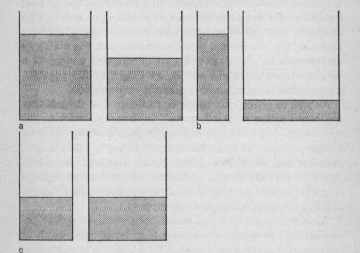

Figure 6

The children were asked to judge which glass contained more water, the amounts actually differing in all cases. It was found, as predicted, that children who had achieved conservation took longer to make a judgement about pair b than about pairs a and c, since both the diameter of the glasses and the water levels in them differed in pair b, and only one or the other varied in pairs a and c. Similarly, as expected, nonconservers did not differ in their judgement times for pairs a and b; if account is being taken only of one factor, the judgement in the case of pair b may be made as easily as that for pair a. For the same reason, it was predicted that non-conservers would make an equally quick judgement in the case of pair c, where there is a difference only in the width of the glasses. Most non-conservers, however, took longer over this judgement, apparently because they were trying carefully to establish whether the water levels, and hence quantities, were precisely equal, an interpretation supported by incorrect judgements ('the same') and verbal statements. Clough concluded that children who take account of only one aspect, fix on height only and not sometimes on height and sometimes on diameter. Patterns of response time of older non-conserving children in a transitional phase suggested that the ability to compensate for differences in two dimensions undergoes a progressive development and is, as Piaget (1952) suggests, important in the attainment of quantity conservation.

As well as giving reasons for equivalence that suggest they are coordinating spatial features, children also refer to the previous equivalence and to the fact that nothing has been added or taken away in the interval (Piaget, 1952; Piaget, Inhelder and Szeminska, 1960). Piaget and Inhelder (1969) maintain that the second argument (nothing added or subtracted) involves a higher level of reasoning and they cite the results of a longitudinal study in support.

Whether or not children attain conservation by first co-ordinating two spatial dimensions (e.g. height and width or area covered and distance between objects), it is an important question in itself how they come to realize that a change in one spatial relation involves compensatory changes in others.

In the conservation experiments, the two spatial relations that are compared in two differing arrangements may be perceived together. When one of two sets of objects that were arranged in similar patterns is spread out over a larger area, the two arrangements may still be seen at once. When, however, a spatial layout has to be conceived from a different viewpoint, from that which is seen, a transposition of the objects relative to the subject has to be made. Piaget and Inhelder (1956) report a study in which children were given a lay-out of a model of three mountains and three similar objects with which to copy the model. When facing it, younger children could reproduce the relations as they were, the brown one to the left of the green one and the yellow one behind both. If, however, they were asked to imagine the view as seen by someone 180 degrees opposite and to place the mountains as they would be seen from there, they were unable to do this; equally, they were unable to do it as looked at 90 degrees round on either side. The more advanced started reversing the fore–aft or the left–right relation of one pair of objects, but they ended up with the objects as in the view that faced them at the moment. Similarly, when given photographs of the mountains from various viewpoints, they selected that which was facing them at the moment. Later in childhood the arrangement is correctly reproduced from any imagined viewpoint.

In addition to having difficulty in coordinating two spatial relations, children, when they are about five years old, have a similar problem in relating guesses as to the identity of different parts of a blurred picture, in attempts to identify the whole picture (Potter, in Bruner *et al.*, 1966).

Others of the Harvard studies indicate, too, that by the age of seven years or so, children relate two hypotheses, in contrast to younger ones who propose unrelated ones. Using a 'Twenty Questions' game, for instance, Mosher and Hornsby (in Bruner *et al.*, 1966) reported that nearly all the younger children asked a series of questions that were unrelated to one another by anything other than an associative connection that did not aid in the task of discovering which of an array of pictures the experimenter had in mind: over half of the eight year olds in contrast to younger children asked more general questions that extracted information they could make use of when they asked the next one. These referred to common features of two or more pictures, asking whether 'it' (the picture to be discovered) had feature x. A positive or negative answer in this case can then be utilized to infer which pictures to eliminate and which to retain, and to frame the next question accordingly. The questions of younger children (e.g. 'Is it the hammer?') can yield no such information.

With the problem, described in the last chapter, of finding which of two or three patterns was correct, a 'marked change' is reported, beginning with the seven-year-old group (Olson, 1966). The task was to find which given pattern was 'correct', by pressing bulbs which lit up when they corresponded with spots of the patterns displayed above on a bulb-board. In one condition, the 'free' one, the children were left to their own devices; in the other, the 'constrained' condition, they were asked, after each press, which button they were going to press next. The developmental change, which appeared first in the constrained condition, was to adopt the most economical strategy, of pressing bulbs which gave information and of using this to guide the selection of the next bulb to be pressed. For example, if two patterns were a T and an L, to press a bulb on the common vertical stroke would give no information as to the 'correct' pattern: to press a bulb, either along the top line of the T or the lower line of the L, would give information as to which was correct. If the L was correct and a bulb of the cross-bar of the T had been pressed, the fact that it did not light up would give the necessary information for inferring that the L was correct. The problem could be solved with one press. When there were three patterns, information of a negative kind, if a certain bulb were pressed, could be utilized to eliminate one pattern and consequently to determine which bulb to press to decide between the other two patterns.

This is thus a matter of relating two comparisons. Inhelder and Piaget (1964) and Piaget, Inhelder and Szeminska (1960) make the same point with regard to measurement, seriation and classification. Concerning measurement, they maintain that it requires inferring a relation of equality between the instrument, B, and the first section measured, A (A = B), and between the instrument and the next section measured, C, (B = C) and from this inferring that A = C. Their observations were of spontaneous measurement. The use of a unit in the form of a stick shorter than the model to be stepped along it was a relatively late development, after seven or eight years.

With regard to seriation, the behaviour of five-year-old children, when they are given a set of graded sticks to place in order of size, was described in the last chapter. They may, for example, select any one, compare it with the last one placed, discard the one taken and select another, until one comparison satisfies some 'test' of the child, whereupon they leave that stick in their arrangement.

Selection of a set of sticks in order of size does not necessarily imply an understanding of seriation. Piaget (1952) has pointed out that this is a matter of realizing that each element has only one place in the series, where it is more than those before it and less than those after it. The way the child goes about inserting an element is more revealing of what he understands. It is only the first step to compare the element to be inserted with *one* in the arranged set. This only indicates whether the element goes before or after the one with which it is compared, but not how far; further comparisons with elements in that direction are necessary to find the exact place.

Up to a certain point in development children find the task of inserting a second set of sticks more difficult than arranging the first set in order. Nevertheless, observation of the inserting actions does not provide unambiguous information, particularly if both sets increase by equal amounts. It is possible that children are making a perceptual judgement of the amount of the difference between adjacent sticks when they move a stick along from one end until they find its place.

The child's processes are more clearly brought out in behaviour when he is instructed to insert weights into a set he has put in order. Since the differences between successive weights cannot be visually judged, some children compare the inserted weight (all are of the same volume) with only one other before placing it; it is easy to distinguish this behaviour from that of children who go on to make a second comparison. In this case the element to be inserted is compared with one in the series, for example, the third. It is then compared with another, the second or fourth; the direction of the difference of the first comparison indicates whether to move up or down the series for the second comparison. Similarly, the outcome of the two comparisons, both in the same direction or one less than and one more than, indicates the next correct action: to make a further comparison with another element in the same direction or to place the new element between the last two that were compared. The investigation of the seriation of length might be better conducted in conditions which prevent the child from making an intuitive judgement on the basis of seeing the trend. This could be achieved if the ordered set of sticks were hidden in a box and the child had to take one out in order to compare those to be inserted with it.

There are similar problems in finding satisfactory behavioural criteria for determining when the child can relate two classes when one is included in the other. Handling the relation of class-inclusion means recognizing that each element is at one and the same time a member of a subclass and of the general class that includes it, by virtue of different attributes in each case. It follows that any general class has more members than any of its subclasses.

Inhelder and Piaget (1964) have made the most comprehensive study of the process by which children come to classify with an understanding of class-inclusion. They maintain that for a certain period up to about seven or eight years, children forget the general class as soon as they divide it into subclasses and, similarly, forget the latter when they combine them into a more general one. Handling the relation of class-inclusion means holding the results of both operations of combining and separating, and recognizing that one is the inverse of the other. Vygotsky (1962), in his pioneering study many years ago, pointed out that successful sorting by one criterion of a set of objects clearly does not provide the necessary information for determining whether the child understands class-inclusion. Inhelder and Piaget (1964) devised a number of techniques for dealing with this problem, some of which were used by Lovell, Mitchell and Everett (1962) in a replicatory study. These cannot be described in detail here. One example will suffice to illustrate the distinction that is being made.

Children were presented with a set of objects such as flowers or beads. Beads were in two colours, for example, blue and white, and all were made of wood; there were more of one colour than the other, for example, more blue than white. The children were instructed to imagine necklaces made of the beads and were asked whether one made of wooden beads would be longer or shorter than one made of white beads. The replies of younger children suggested they were comparing the two collections they could see, those of white beads and blue beads, while beyond the age of seven or eight years, the majority appeared to be comparing the whole class of wooden beads with a subclass of blue ones. Elkind (1961) replicated one variant of this task, asking about the number of boys, girls and children in their class, with similar results. Inhelder and Piaget (1964) investigated the problem further by asking children such questions as 'Are all the blue ones square?', when a collection contained various forms and colours, and by observing the way children made hierarchical classifications.

Classifying requires the individual to deal simultaneously with *groups* of objects which cannot be seen together at the same time in different groupings. Similarly, the application of number involves reference to a group of objects and simple arithmetical operations involve the relation of two or more numbers which have such a reference. Children who can count a row of objects accurately (as most can by five years) cannot, however, think in terms of a group of objects, let alone relate two such groups. Reference was made earlier to one of the Genevan conservation studies in which liquid from one of two identical glasses is poured into a third of a different shape. When the liquid has been poured back, the procedure is to pour it again into two or four glasses and the child is asked about the equivalence of the liquid in one of the original glasses and that in the four smaller ones. Some children have difficulty in making a comparison between the quantities in *one* larger glass and *four* smaller ones. When they reply, they often point to *one* of the smaller glasses, which of course contains less liquid than the larger glass. If the investigator indicates the whole set and repeats the question they show a lack of comprehension.

If the child is unable to think in terms of a group of objects at once, it seems unlikely that when he speaks a number, for example, five, he is referring to a group of five objects. It may instead be the case that the number, the verbal label, is only another name for the object – albeit for the objects as touched successively. This raises the question of what psychological processes are involved in enumeration. Little analysis appears to have been made of this. Learning the sequence of number names is clearly necessary, but by no means sufficient. Young pre-school children can learn long sequences of words, if given sufficient practice – and many parents ensure that this is given with regard to the number sequence! Whether in overt speech and action or implicitly, counting requires the coordination of verbal and motor systems, of the pronunciation of a number name at the same time as touching, pointing at or looking at an object. Before they can achieve this, younger children at times pronounce two number names while touching one object or touch two while speaking one number. Many, however, by the age of five years, coordinate speech and touching when confronted with a row of objects. It may be that they have achieved nothing more than verbal–motor coordination and have no concept of number as referring to a group of objects.

Enumeration of a scattered group of objects requires more than the verbal–motor coordination. It requires a systematic approach, in order to ensure that all the objects are included and that none is counted twice. When objects are in some regular arrangement, such as a row, or matrix of columns and rows, or a triangle, a system is given, though Beckwith and Restle (1966) have pointed out that circles and squares pose problems of stop-rules. So also does the task of copying the order of beads, presented in a circular arrangement, onto a rod, a linear arrangement. Children of five and six years succeed in doing this (Lovell, 1959; Piaget and Inhelder, 1956), and severely subnormal children and adults who do not conserve quantity with continuous liquids or discrete objects, or show evidence of seriation, also succeed with the above task (Woodward, 1962a). Children in this period thus presumably adopt some strategy for dealing with the stop-rule problem. It might be expected also that they would deal with it when enumerating objects in a regular arrangement in which a system is thereby given. When objects are scattered, however, no such system is given and the subject has to adopt one himself by, for example, removing each one from the collection as it is counted. Beckwith and Restle (1966) found that seven-year-old children took longer to count a scattered arrangement than a circular or rectangular one and made more errors with it.

It might be postulated that the adoption of a systematic approach in enumerating would be a concurrent, or almost concurrent, development with the others that occur at about seven years, since it implies that the child considers the whole set of elements and adopts a plan (or strategy) to deal with them, as does the conservation of quantities, classifying, serializing and coordinating spatial relations.

Thus one question that is raised by these changes around the age of seven years is whether children give prior consideration to a group of objects as a whole, before they act to interrelate them on the basis of attributes and spatial relations; related to this is the question of the ability to coordinate two abstracted features, such as classes, relations, dimensions and hypotheses. This brings us to a discussion of the processes that are involved in these changes.

Prior analysis and precision

It may be as well, first, to summarize the various changes that have been described. We have seen that some time in their early school years children are able to classify a set of objects consistently and also to change the basis of that classification in order to deal with a new situation of additional elements that do not fit into the existing classification, instead of hanging on to their first criterion. They are able to relate three elements in a series, instead of only two at a time. They are able to separate quantity, length, etc., from the spatial arrangements of the elements or the containers, to take account of compensatory changes in a second spatial relation when one is made in the first; objects looked at from the opposite viewpoint will not only be reversed in terms of their fore and aft positions, but also in their left–right relations. In addition, children show evidence of relating successive hypotheses about different parts of a complex whole, of seeking information in a form that enables them to make an inference, as a basis for the next step taken.

It should be emphasized that this is not a complete list of all the developmental changes that occur around the seventh and eighth years, but only an attempt to give representative examples of a number of them. Hence to look for common features among them may be misleading, if a generalization is made beyond those that have been discussed.

In all of these the child appears to have moved from handling one comparison, rule or hypothesis to handling two, and relating them. Piaget and Inhelder have drawn attention to the seven year old's capacity to relate two classes, two relations of difference and two dimensions, spatial or temporal. The Harvard group have produced results concerning the child's ability to relate two hypotheses or the outcomes of two judgements. It should also be stressed, as Lunzer (1960) has pointed out, that the difference is comparing two judgements, compared with earlier making a single judgement, comparing two *things* and, moreover, deriving an appropriate conclusion from the compared judgements.

How is the child now able to do this? Must some new, higher order process in the organism be postulated? If so, what has contributed to its development?

Piaget and Inhelder advance the concept of operational structures. One kind of concrete operations (the 'logico-arithmetical') deal with the attributes of discrete objects: in classifying and serial ordering, the spatial location of the objects and occurrence in time are irrelevant. The other kind (spatio-temporal) deal with the spatial and temporal relations between a field of objects or within the parts of a single object, with continua, not discrete objects. The first kind thus includes numerical operations, the second the measurement of continua. The main feature of 'operativity' is reversibility: a result can be undone. Adding two numbers or combining two classes into a more general one can be undone, with a return to the starting point of the original numbers or classes. This passing to and from one state to the other makes it possible to retain both and hence to examine relations between them. Overt action can achieve only one state or the other; another *action* has then to be performed to get back to the starting point. Reversible operational systems make it possible to conserve the invariance of quantities, etc., through various transformations into different states.

The conservations illustrate a different form of reversibility, that of reciprocity or compensation. The child who refers to the increase in the distance between objects, as well as the increase in the area they cover, is showing this form of reversibility, as is the child who refers to the smaller diameter of a glass in which the water level rises higher.

Bruner (1964, and in Bruner *et al.*, 1966) regarded the developmental change as one in the mode of representation. Having advanced beyond action in his second year, the child then uses an 'ikonic' mode, or imagery. This is static: things can be remembered only as they are given and perceived. The Bruner and Kenney matrix of beakers can be reproduced in the given arrangement, with the same point of origin, but not when the point or origin is moved to a different corner. The greater flexibility required by this is given by a new 'symbolic' mode of representation, mainly but not entirely linguistic. For example, the child uses relational terms (e.g. 'gets fatter') to describe the relations among the set of beakers. The child who achieves conservation recognizes the contradiction between his successive statements that two equivalent quantities are the same and that one is greater than the other.

Whether or not the main feature is such use of language or other symbolic forms, it is undoubtedly an important step to describe precisely the relations that are observed between sets of events and objects, such as changes in two dimensions.

The point of difference between Piaget and Bruner is in whether such use of language is essential for analysing the features common to a set of objects, or the spatial relations among a set, or to relate two successive comparisons. It is not proposed to enter into this controversy here. The interested reader will find discussions of it in the respective publications (Bruner, 1964, and in Bruner *et al.*, 1966; Inhelder, Bovet, Sinclair and Smock, 1966; Sinclair-de-Zwart, 1969; see also Furth, 1964). It is proposed instead to consider psychological processes, such as selective attending to relevant features, and a memory factor, in the development of what appears to be a trend towards greater precision, and analysis, for Bruner also agreed that there must be prior developments before language can be used in this way.

It may be argued that the 'conserver' is not exactly perceiving the world differently, in the sense that things are seen as bigger or smaller in different contexts, as with visual illusions. What he does do is pay attention to other parts of it that he previously ignored, while still attending to the features he looked at before. This is most clearly brought out when children are asked to *judge* the equality or difference of two quantities without having been given evidence first of this equivalence. The study of Clough, quoted earlier, demonstrates this.

Piaget has drawn attention to this feature, of the extension of selective attending to relevant aspects, under the concept of 'decentration'. The 'pre-operational' child centres on one aspect of the situation. This is most fully discussed with regard to judgements in psychophysical experiments, and the developmental changes in the extent to which children are subject to illusions are attributed to decentration (Piaget, 1961).

When a *group* of objects is involved, as for instance in classifying and seriating, does the child who relates two classes, or spatial relations, or differences, etc., consider the interrelations among all the elements or the parts of a whole before acting to classify, make a selective comparison, etc.? Is this one of the advances made over earlier behaviour?

Children of five years appear unable to consider a group as a whole in terms of some abstracted feature, let alone to relate two such features, each defining the group in a different way. This is most clearly evident where children cannot comprehend a comparison between the contents of four small glasses, taken together, and one larger one. Such comprehension would seem to be necessary for the understanding of number and for the relation of numbers in simple arithmetical operations. Similarly the concept of one class of objects defined by a common property would seem to be a necessary prior development to the interrelation of two classes.

Inhelder and Piaget (1964) have devised problems to investigate the question of the prior interrelation of the attributes with regard to seriating and classifying. The argument, in the case of classifying, was based on the way children altered the basis of their classification when new elements were added. From this they inferred that the children were taking account of the interrelations in the set as a whole.

Prior analysis may be inferred when children in the Olson study pressed an informative bulb: if the patterns were a T and an inverted T, to avoid pressing a bulb along the common vertical line and to press one on one of the horizontal lines seems to indicate that an analysis was made of lines that were and were not common to both patterns. The Bruner and Kenney matrix of beakers would also seem to require such analysis for success in the transposed condition.

The essential feature in this prior looking over a set of elements for relations among them would seem to be the greater precision of the analysis: of the attributes and how they may be interrelated, of the variable by which elements may be ordered, of common features in two arrays or diagrams, of the effect of a change in one spatial relation upon another. If a sequence of actions is performed in accordance with the analysis and decision this would seem to require the postulate of a higher order plan that guides the sequence of actions.

A second question that may be raised concerning the 'seven-year-change' is the role of a memory factor, bearing in mind that what is held is the result of two comparisons, not merely a sequence of words or numbers. The study of Olson (1966), which has already been described, provided some evidence that younger children tend to 'lose' the result of the first outcome or comparison. For example, one child dealing with the problem of discovering which of three patterns was correct, pressed a button which gave him the information that either pattern 1 or pattern 2 was correct, but not 3. The second bulb he pressed gave him the information that either pattern 2 or 3 was correct. It was then possible to infer that 2 was the correct pattern, since 3 had been excluded by the first press. The child went on, however, to press four more 'informative bulbs' before he solved the problem. In all his presses, he adopted the most advanced 'informative' strategy of selecting bulbs which would give information about excluding a pattern, but he was unable to relate the two results of his selective actions.

Thus, it might be postulated that an increase in immediate memory plays an important part in the 'seven-year change'. Indeed McLaughlin (1963) has pointed to correspondences between increases in the 'immediate memory span' for digits and the beginning of the stages distinguished by Piaget.

Wetherick and Freeland (1969) also pointed to a short-term memory factor in a developmental change in primary-school children, in connection with the ability to hold the common feature extracted from one set of elements, while eliminating others.

A third possible factor contributing to the change is an increase in flexibility. This has been proposed by both Piaget and Bruner. Piaget and Inhelder regard increased flexibility as important in the development of operational systems. Instances of such flexibility are taking account of the outcome of a previous erroneous action to modify a subsequent one and, particularly, of taking account of a possible outcome, before action, in order to avoid errors (Inhelder and Piaget, 1964). Bruner (in Bruner *et al.*, 1966) contrasts the static image with the mobility of more precise verbal coding.

Thus it is postulated that the child gets beyond the inflexibility in action and imagery either by making abstractions from his actions upon objects (Piaget and Inhelder) or by the use of a more highly developed symbolic system (Bruner). It is possible that both may be operative. The 'seven-year change' may involve both a new form of coding, for more precise description and storage, and new processing systems for making the analysis. If so, investigation is required of the interrelations between them, as well as the study of the development of each. This monograph has been concerned with the interrelations of action and central processing systems, rather than with the development of imagery and of verbal coding systems. It will thus go on to consider the question of how these higher order systems develop from action, from dual-choice behavioural sequences. How do these retroactive, step-by-step behavioural sequences become higher order systems that can operate upon classes and numbers (derived from sets of objects) and upon the results of comparisons? How do actions that relate two objects by an attribute or spatial relation develop into systems that relate a set of objects by their features? How does irreversible overt action develop into Piaget's reversible 'mental operations'? This seems, on the face of it, to be more of a difference than that discussed at the end of chapter 4, from sensorimotor sequences of actions and sensory feedback from them, to the coordination of actions before their performance.

The relation of a sequence of actions and feedback to higher central processes has been raised in connection with the explanation of the rapid execution of movements in highly skilled sequences, and this postulated relation has been referred to in discussions of the development of central mediating processes, for example, by Bruner (in Bruner *et al.*, 1966) and Osgood (1953). Lashley (1951), in a paper which is often quoted in this context, pointed out that in highly skilled sequences, as when a musician plays notes in rapid succession, the movements succeed one another too quickly for there to be time for sensory feedback from each movement to provide the cue for the next one, as there is during learning when the movements are slower. Consequently a postulate is required of some central process that activates the various muscles in the order that is appropriate for the performance.

At one level this is a matter of specifying the details of the neurophysiological process and this, of course, is the problem that Hebb (1949) tackled so comprehensively. At a less specific level it requires postulating no more than a central process that produces the performance of the sequence of actions in the order in which they were previously performed. The same sequence of actions is being carried out in rapid succession as when the skill was being learned, when the sequence was performed more slowly.

The operations of thinking that we are now considering, and their relation to performance, are more complex than the rapid execution of movement. The neural system cannot be conceived of as a 'copy' of the sequence of actions if the operations are different in kind from the actions.

One of the main points made by Piaget and Inhelder is that thinking can accomplish that which is impossible in action; for example, a general class and the subclasses it contains can be thought of simultaneously, while action can produce only one or the other arrangement at a time.

The gap between action and feedback, on the one hand, and 'operational' systems or higher order plans, on the other, thus seems large, with an explanation in terms of 'autonomous central processes' (Hebb, 1949), difficult. If, however, the process in operational classifying and so forth were the implicitly rapid performance of the same actions that were previously performed in overt behaviour, such an explanation would be tenable. Piaget and Inhelder (1956) appear, in fact, to have suggested that this is what actually occurs. 'To arrange objects mentally is not merely to imagine a series of things already set out in order, nor even to imagine the action of arranging them. It means arranging the series, just as positively and actively as if the action were physical, but performing the action internally on symbolic objects' (p. 454).

The 'units' upon which internal operations such as classifying, adding, measuring and so on, are performed, are *groups* of symbolic objects or events defined by common features, numbers, spatial and temporal relations, etc.; actions are performed upon single objects. If operating with these higher units is achieved through the rapid execution, in 'implicit' form, of the previous overt actions, something in the nature of a hierarchical structure of processes within the organism emerges, similar to the hierarchical structure of behaviour which is indicated by the detailed description and analysis of behavioural sequences. A plan, defined as a hierarchical process within the organism that controls the order of a sequence of operations (actions or mental operations), is of this nature. The higher order, implicit, 'mental' operations to be discussed next would then be conceived of as a yet higher level in the hierarchical structure, the subunits being the operations of classifying, serializing, adding, relating spatial dimensions, etc. We are here firmly in the realm of speculation. Piaget, however (particularly in Inhelder and Piaget, 1958) supports such a hypothesis concerning hierarchical structures by a logical analysis of the operations performed, indicated by the behaviour that is elicited by suitable problems.

We now turn to an analysis of the way children tackle these problems.

Testing hypotheses

It should be emphasized again that the problem situation, the inferred central processes and behaviour, are being considered as an indissoluble whole, the last two interacting in the course of the solution of the problem. The process of reasoning is thus not being considered in isolation, nor is overt behaviour regarded only as a means of gaining information about the nature of the process of thinking, of externalizing the process. The focus of interest is in the way that action is taken to obtain information of a kind that will allow an inference to be made by the individual concerning complex interrelations between events.

We have seen, in the Olson study, that when children are instructed to stop and consider before each move they make, seven year olds can take selective action to decide between two alternatives and perform another selective action on the basis of the outcome of the first, then coming to a conclusion by relating the two outcomes. This was not, however, common until the age of nine years, in the condition in which children were not asked each time which button to press next. If more factors have to be taken into account, it is much later, in earlier or later adolescence, that selective actions are taken such that an unambiguous conclusion may be drawn from the results of them. For example, Inhelder and Piaget (1958) set children the task of discovering the variables that influence the flexibility of rods. The material consisted of a set of rods that differed in diameter, the form of the cross-section and the material they were made of. Length could be varied by placing the rod at different points in a clamp and weights of different values were available to be placed on the tip of the rods.

The rods were compared two at a time. Children between seven and eleven years or so, who could classify and serialiate, differed from adolescents in their selection of rods for comparison. The younger selected any two rods and compared them; they observed the results and ranked the rods in order for degrees of bending. They thus observed first and ordered afterwards. They also apparently did not realize that a comparison of two rods that differed in more than one factor (e.g. material and thickness) was useless. In contrast to this, older children selected rods for comparison that were equal in all respects but one, for example, material. They could then arrive at a conclusion as to the role of the factor that they varied, depending on whether the rods bent to the same extent or by a different amount. The comparison *to be made* thus influenced a series of selective actions of this kind.

This leads us to examine, in contrast to earlier behaviour, the number of prior 'tests' that have to be made, namely, the number of comparisons that have to be made and inter-related, and whether this can be done without a systematic approach.

We may compare first the operations of adolescents with the above problem and those involved when an element is inserted in a series. When five variables have to be examined, five successive comparisons have to be made, the results remembered or recorded and interrelated. In contrast, when an element is inserted in a series, only two successive comparisons have to be made and the results held and interrelated.

The operations in the rods problem may also be contrasted with those in sorting and classifying. The child who selects two rods that are the same in four respects, and different in a fifth, is doing something much more complex than selecting an object from an array that is the same colour as one that is separate or even sorting by successive dual-choice actions. This requires only the selection of an object by the same attribute as in the previous match, and the specific match within it. It is not necessary even to determine in how many features the objects vary. The selection of the two rods, to be equal in all respects but one, requires the identification of all the variables and then making five successive comparisons, checking that four yield a result of equality and one of difference. This is a sequence of five 'tests' before the comparison of the two rods for flexibility is made. This comparison for flexibility is only one in a series that has to be made, before the final conclusion is drawn from the interrelation of all these comparisons. There are, then, more levels of operating and testing than in classifying and serializing.

This procedure is, of course, one of those used in scientific investigation. It requires, moreover, not only making a sequence of several 'tests' and judgements before making *each* of a *series* of comparisons; it is necessary also to ensure that all the variables have been examined and thereby eliminated as irrelevant or retained as relevant. By the age of seven years or so children can check through a list of features in two pictures before judging them to be the same. Vurpillot (1968) examined the strategies that children of different ages used before they pronounced two pictures to be the same or different. The determination of difference, of course, requires that a difference in only one feature need be found; the existence of others does not matter. Before a judgement of 'same' can be made, all the features have to be compared in turn and checked off as the same. Vurpillot used pairs of house-fronts, each with three rows of two windows. They differed or were alike in the presence or absence of shutters, plant-pot, a light, etc. Eye movements were recorded. Younger children tended to state similarity without checking through all the possible features, once they had seen similarity in one. Comparison of pairs of features began to appear among the five year olds and was consistent among the six year olds.

Once this comparison of features has been carried out and the judgement of 'same' or 'different' made, the result may be forgotten when the next two pictures are examined. The task does not require that the successive judgements be related. When the task is to determine which variables produce an event, as in the rods problem, such linking is required. The whole sequence may then be regarded as a coordinated, higher order one, incorporating lower level operations of the kind in the Vurpillot study.

Moreover, the subject has to organize the sequence of comparisons himself; they are not presented to him. This means that he has to adopt some strategy for ensuring that each variable is examined and that none is examined twice. This, too, is comparable, at a higher level, to adopting the strategy of a systematic approach to ensure, in enumerating a scattered collection, that every one is counted and once only.

In a 'matching' problem, Donaldson (1963) found that one source of error in children of around eleven years was to fail to consider all possible alternatives; they thus concluded that one was correct without having eliminated all alternatives. The problem was to match five boys to five schools on the basis of the information given. This consisted of four statements of the following kinds: no. 1 does not go to schools A, B and C; no. 2 goes to school D; no. 3 does not go to schools A or C; and no. 4 has never been inside school C. The fifth school was not specifically mentioned in the four statements, though it was named in the introductory statement, and the information was sufficient for solution of the problem. The fifth school was most frequently ignored when erroneous conclusions were drawn. An example of failure to consider all alternatives is the following: 'He doesn't go to North, South or Central (A, B or C) schools, so he goes to West.'

The question of whether children systematically consider and combine all possible alternatives has been examined by Inhelder and Piaget (1958) with a probem designed for the purpose. They used five glasses containing different chemicals. When samples from three were poured into one glass, a yellow mixture was produced. Some liquid from one other neutralized the colour and the fifth contained water which produced no change. The most economical approach is the systematic combination of all possible pairs and then of sets of three; solution is difficult without a system. (Once the effect is obtained, the other combinations are not, of course, run through.) A further step is to discover the role of water and, finally, to take action to test the hypothesis that it is water. Inhelder and Piaget report that such testing occurred towards the age of fifteen and sixteen years, though a systematic approach was common earlier. Leskow and Smock (1970) similarly found a change in this age group in the ability to handle permutations systematically.

Inhelder and Piaget do not distinguish between the systematic comparison of all combinations of two and of all combinations of three. The first would seem, however, to be less complex. The systematic combination of each element with every other in a set of five elements may be achieved by comparing the first with each of the others, then the second one with the third, fourth and fifth, the third with the fourth and fifth, and so on. In order to compare three at a time systematically, it is necessary to keep track of the system of combinations of two, along with the system of combining a third with each of the combinations of two. In the comparison of pairs, the first element has to be held or retained in memory only until it has been compared with each of the others; then it can be forgotten. So, too, with each of the other elements. When comparing three, it is the *combination* of two that has to be held until it has been compared with each of the others – and so on with each combination of two. Thus, before the first step can be taken, the pair of, for example, one and two has to be combined and held while it is combined with the third, fourth and fifth. Before the next step in the combining of three can be taken, the second combination of the system of two has to be performed; the first and third have to be combined and held while this pair is combined with the fourth and fifth. Thus it is necessary to keep track of two systems simultaneously and at each step in the next feedback loop a change in each system has to be made. Once this has been made there is a change in one system, until each member has been run through.

In the problems discussed so far the subject is required to observe the results of actions that are guided by the subsequent reasoning operations to be performed. The results of these observations have to be held while relations between them are examined. Inhelder and Piaget (1958) have also drawn attention to the fact that, some time in adolescence, problems are solved when compensatory interrelations are given and have to be taken into account. The seven year old's handling of compensatory changes in two spatial relations or dimensions has been described. Children cannot, however, handle three until several years later. Piaget, Inhelder and Szeminska (1960) report a study in which children were presented with a structure made of cubes (a 'house' with a given number of 'rooms'). They were instructed to build another house, with the same number of rooms, on a base of a different area. For example, a model on a base of 3×3 cubes and four cubes high had to be reproduced on a base of 2×2 or 2×3. The qualitative comparison of the areas and some increase in height to compensate for the smaller area, achieved by younger children, are steps on the way; solution with the exact relation worked out was not common until eleven and twelve years.

A similar change was found with regard to the handling of direct and inverse proportion, though children of nine and ten years again achieved a qualitative compensation (Inhelder and Piaget, 1958; Piaget and Inhelder, 1956). Among the problems used for the study of the child's understanding of direct proportion was one in which the child was required to draw similar triangles and rectangles. Once children measure length, they presumably could reproduce a rectangle the same size as another. The measurements of the two sides may be treated separately. When a larger or smaller scale one is required, the relation of proportion between the two lengths has to be preserved. The lower level operations of measuring and dividing (or multiplying) are then incorporated in a more complex operation.

For the investigation of the handling of inverse proportion, Inhelder and Piaget (1958) used a task which required children to place rings of different diameters at the appropriate distances from a light source to make their shadows on a screen coincide. With a second problem the experimenter hung a weight on one arm of a horizontal bar, thus making it tip up. The child was given a weight of a different value and set the task of making the bar horizontal again by placing the weight on the other arm. The solution of the exact inverse relation was achieved relatively late with both problems, though with the second problem children of eight to ten years could solve the problem if both weights were equal. In this case they had only to equate two distances and no problem of proportion was involved.

Piaget and Inhelder (1958) report a study in which children were given a bowl of water and a set of various objects. They were instructed to classify the objects into those that would sink and those that would float, and they were then shown what happened. Further inquiry then sought to discover the basis of their classification and their modification in the face of contradictory evidence. The inconsistent, unrelated statements of five- and six-year-old children are similar to those reported by Bruner *et al.* (1966). For example, children predicted that a plank of wood would sink, because 'it is heavy' or because 'it is big'. When they saw that it floated, they gave some such reason as 'it's bigger' or 'it comes back up'. The explanation of why a wooden ball comes up may then be that it is smaller. Similarly, the statement that heavy things sink and light things float cannot be brought to terms with the evidence of the floating of a heavy piece of wood and the sinking of a pin. The seven to nine year olds made some advance towards relating weight and volume rather than speaking of absolute size or weight, but it was more often the older children (eleven or twelve years onwards) who began to relate the weight of the object to the weight of the water and then to move on to the weight of water of the same volume as the object. When asked to prove their assertions, they spoke of using containers of the same volume and of weighing the contents (water and the object).

To use this kind of problem for experimental purposes runs the risk of contamination from teaching in secondary school science and some statements quoted in the published protocols have a ring of this about them. However, Lovell (1961) replicated most of the studies reported by Inhelder and Piaget on adolescent thinking and found that he could distinguish between the repetition of a verbal statement, learned by rote, and the understanding of the principle. Furthermore, he reports that some children who had not had formal teaching on the principle concerned could discover it themselves, given the appropriate materials.

Concerning changes in the process of reasoning itself, Inhelder and Piaget (1958) argue that the important change in adolescence, compared with middle childhood, is to be able to reason with hypothetical statements of the possible, instead of being restricted to that which could exist in concrete form. Secondly, the necessary implication of one statement for another is recognized. The tying of the thinking of children from seven to about eleven years to concrete forms is shown up clearly by a study in a different Genevan work (Piaget and Inhelder, 1956). Interest was in the child's concepts of a point and continuity. The children were instructed to bisect a line and then to draw another half the length of that half, and so on until the line was too small for further subdivision. It was then suggested that they should continue this process in imagination. Then the idea of subdividing squares, triangles, circles, etc., was introduced. Children of under about eleven years could continue the process in imagination, but they held to the shape of the original form, while older children more often conceived of a point. The adolescents could also conceive of infinite subdivision.

These findings raise questions about intermediate steps, such as conceiving of a class of objects beyond the members present; of conceiving of the possibility of interpolating elements in a series, when not actually offered any to insert; of whether the concept of continua arises from each extrapolation and interpolations of discrete objects.

Although far from exhaustive, the examples that have been given may serve to illustrate the differences between children who can handle two relations and those who can simultaneously handle three or more and use the lower order operations in a more complex sequence, this then constituting a higher order one. In the examples discussed, the individual has to make a number of comparisons and hold them while other operations are performed and examine the interrelations and implications. Similarly when a test is made of various alternative hypotheses, it is necessary to remember which ones have been eliminated and which have still to be considered. The role of a memory factor is again raised. Donaldson (1963) found that 'loss of hold' appeared to be one feature in the errors of some children in problem solving.

Concluding comments

With thinking by implication and actions organized in such a way as to test hypotheses, we have reached the end-point that was proposed at the beginning of this monograph. It is, however, evident that the gap between the reflexes and undirected movements of the neonate and adult processes of thinking is far from closed. This monograph has not attempted to close it; it has merely aimed to discuss the classification of different forms of organized behaviour, which may be taken as stepping stones that may serve as orienting points for asking further questions.

The account has concentrated on organized behaviour that is directed towards the discovery of principles that govern events in the environment or towards understanding an exposition of them. It has entirely neglected artistic productions and aesthetic appreciation. The early behavioural sequences that lead to the central operations that are involved in these are equally open to analysis. Questions concerning this would again direct attention to the rearrangements of objects that children make, on the basis of such features as colour and form; interest would, however, be in arrangements that are regular but not in a classificatory or serializing manner. Attention would also be directed to observation of the actions that children make upon objects that produce sounds with regularities and of the rearrangements they make of words in a formal and metaphorical manner. The difference between the strumming on a string or the imaginative play of a pre-school child and the production of a symphony or literary work is as great as that between the young child's attempts to 'see how it works' by pulling it to pieces and the discoveries of scientists.

A further point that has not been discussed is whether yet higher levels of organization occur in adult life or whether any further developments are elaborations of the systems developed in adolescence. When the number of all possible combinations is too vast to be run through, adults adopt strategies to deal with the situation. The exploration of this question requires the comparison of young adults and adolescents. Rayner (1958), who observed strategies used in a game of 'peggity', found that adults, compared with adolescents, took much longer over each move; they also showed more foresight in using strategies that were sure to win further back from the end of the game, in terms of the number of moves.

The final theoretical point to be taken up is that which was deferred when S. H. White's (1965) paper was discussed. His views concerning the role of the inhibition of the most readily available response, in favour of a less readily available one, were described. In his theoretical interpretation White made a further suggestion: in each of the individual developmental changes between five and seven years, the earlier learning, before the transition, is characterized by an associative learning process and that after it by a higher level of function, which might be termed 'cognitive' or 'reflective'. This higher kind depends 'critically upon the inhibition of associative function, or, at least, of the response which associative function is capable of determining' (S. H. White, 1965, p. 215).

White thus retained the principle of association in his formulation, pointing out that it has been with us for a long time. There are three possible positions that may be taken concerning explanations in terms of associative principles, in the form of conceptions about stimulus–response relations. One is that they are applicable all through development. Such is the view of Berlyne (1965), who made a detailed analysis, in S–R terms, of behaviour and processes in the course of development, including the most complex adolescent forms.

The opposite alternative is to abandon associative principles altogether, in favour of a concept of a self-regulatory mechanism. This was the view of Miller, Galanter and Pribram (1960) (who also add the concept of plan, or directive principle). Since the publication of the TOTE and plan analysis, and in the same year of Deutsch's (1960) physiological model of a self-regulatory system, variations of one of these or of similar models have been used in further formulations, for example, by Bruner (1968) and by Lunzer (1968). The psychologist who favours this approach will soon have as many models to choose from as has the adherent of the first approach.

The third view is that of Hebb (1960), to the effect that s–r analyses are appropriate for the learning of lower animals and for simple human learning, but not for adult thinking and problem solving. Applied to human development, this would be a position similar to that of White. The only question that would be raised would concern the period of development to which associative principles cease to be applicable and 'cognitive' ones appropriate. A case could be made for the change in the second year, instead of that of the five- to seven-year period as proposed by White.

One point of difference is thus whether the most useful unit for analysing behaviour and central processes is the s r association or some self-regulatory mechanism, such as the TOTE. The other is whether the explanation of the sequencing of overt behaviour and of mental operations in thinking requires any other principle than feedback from the preceding action or operation as the cue for the next one. When the experimental study of thinking began at Wurzburg towards the end of the last century, the influence of an extra-associationist factor was quickly discovered, though attempts were made to contain it within the theoretical framework of the 'association of ideas' that was then current.

There are at present advocates both of an organizing principle, such as plan, and of chains of implicit, or symbolic, stimuli and responses. When Berlyne (1965), however, made the attempt to construct a model of the process in more complex forms of child and adult directed thinking, in terms of such chains, he found it necessary to include something that transforms one unit in the chain into something different, in order to account for logical inference. The units that are transformed are symbolic responses and stimuli, termed 'situational thoughts' by Berlyne; these represent external stimulus situations and are considered to be developed from overt receptor adjusting responses, which change the pattern of sensory input without making any change in the environment. Alternating with these are transformational responses and stimuli. These are assumed to be developed from actions that do make changes in the environment, as when an object is moved, the resulting change in the stimulus situation being fed back. A transformational thought is inserted in between each situational thought, in Berlyne's model, in order to account for the 'legitimate steps' in the process leading to a final solution; these change situational thoughts in the way that action operates upon the environment to change one external stimulus situation into another. Berlyne regards transformational thoughts as equivalent to Piaget's operations.

Different theoretical analyses of complex thinking thus postulate constituents of thinking, the symbols, verbal or otherwise, of external situations and some process for transforming them. The difference thus appears to lie in views about the nature of the latter, a link in a linear chain or a system that is hierarchical in structure. One way of approaching this problem is to examine the behaviour itself, the sequence of actions and feedback from which it is assumed, by theorists of different viewpoints, that transformation processes develop. In this monograph an attempt has been made to do this, on the basis of the analysis of behaviour made by Miller, Galanter and Pribram and of Piaget's observations and analyses of behaviour patterns in infancy. From this a picture emerges of a succession of behaviour patterns, progressively more complex in structure, developed from the preceding kind.

It was then suggested that the components that are sequenced prior to action, when the earliest form of thinking occurs, are the most recently developed behaviour patterns which have the most complex structure, developed by way of intermediate forms from the reflexes and undirected movements of the neonate. A contemporary development, which Piaget regards as interrelated with prior sequencing, is that of new means for 'representing' or storing that which has been observed, in the form of words and of mental imagery.

In this chapter the question has been posed of how higher order transformational systems develop from sequences of action and feedback after this. From the analyses of Piaget and Inhelder it has been suggested that sequences of actions upon collections of objects should be considered rather than single responses made to one of two stimulus objects. Since the transformational systems permit the handling of relations based upon the common features or differences of real or symbolic objects, or upon their arrangement in space, the behavioural sequences to which attention has been directed are those that relate objects on the basis of their attributes or spatial relations.

The view of a hierarchical structure of subsequent higher transformation systems begins to emerge, if the results of these transformations (groups of classified, seriated, enumerated objects or relations in space or time among groups of objects or sequences of events) become the units, or constituents, that are operated upon by other transformational systems – whether further actions in middle childhood are involved in the development of the latter, we do not know. Nor do we know how important is the precise use of language for the description and analysis of interrelations between objects and events, in the way that Bruner postulated. The development of language itself is a question for separate, detailed discussion, as is the issue of the role of the child's own speech in regulatory action, as Luria has suggested.

Both Luria (1961) and S. H. White (1965) invoked the concept of inhibition in order to account for the withholding of impulsive, inappropriate action, and Berlyne (1965) has pointed out that it is a possible factor in the process of the gradual attenuation of overt action until the relevant muscles are involved in only a minimal way. Such a postulate would seem to be required when problem solving appears to involve the prior sequencing of existing sensorimotor schemata.

Thus both the earlier change during the second year and that towards the age of seven years may be interpreted in terms of the inhibition of the immediately evoked sequences of actions, but there is a difference. The suggested explanation of the earlier change requires that the performance of learned behaviour patterns is withheld until the sensorimotor schemata are arranged in the appropriate order for performance. The change around seven years requires the explanation of the development of systems that operate implicitly, the actions from which they develop not necessarily being performed at all. If these systems are 'internalized actions', this means inhibition of the overt action altogether.

At this point, we may perhaps conclude by summarizing the aims of the monograph and the main themes that have been discussed in it.

The principle aim has been to introduce the reader to the analysis and classification of complex behaviour and to some of the questions thereby raised.

The main theme is that the study of learning cannot be conducted apart from the developmental perspective if it is to contribute to our knowledge of complex human behaviour and of the central mediating processes that guide it. This has implications for the kinds of question that are asked.

Since development occurs as the result of organism-environment interaction, this means that questions concerning learning are posed in the form of 'What problems does the environment present the child with?' Secondly, questions concerning learning at one period are asked in the light of subsequent learning, in situations in which the child selectively attends to certain features. This requires the detailed analysis of the stimulus situation and of the behavioural sequences performed in it. Moreover, it requires the classification of different forms of behaviour.

The detailed description and analysis of behavioural sequences is of action and sensory feedback, and this entails the inclusion of actions such as looking, listening and touching. This raises two questions concerning the conditions that lead to the repetition and termination of a behavioural sequence, and this in turn raises the issue of self-regulatory processes, since the individual himself sets up the conditions for going on or stopping and he looks for them. The TOTE unit has been regarded as a useful basis for analysis. Some concept, too, would appear to be required to account for the order in which actions and 'central operations' are performed; that of 'plan' has been used.

The classification of different forms of behaviour brings up the problem of the discovery of the appropriate criteria for distinguishing between different forms. Piaget has done most of the pioneering work on this. Nevertheless, there are some periods when behaviour and central processes have not been classified – or when further subdivisions are indicated. In the discussion of the classification of behaviour, sharp distinctions have sometimes been made and it might perhaps be questioned whether this is justifiable on the basis of the present evidence. Again further research will settle the question. This raises another question, that of continuity in development and the validity of classifying behaviour, other than as a temporary strategy, in order to define the questions concerning the detailed, continuous process of change. If we take points in development separated by periods of time, we are able to classify behaviour into different forms. When study is, however, undertaken of the process of change that leads from one form to another, the distinctions may disappear. The point has often been made that, if the process is known in sufficient detail, development is a process of continuous change all through. No one argues the point about continuous, measurable change: the point at issue is in whether or not a different kind of organization, qualitatively distinguishable from the previous one, emerges at a certain point in the process of change. The problem in the study of the development of organized behaviour – and perhaps psychology generally – is that we have not yet found the variables in the process of change. Hence, we do not know what form the measuring instrument will take, nor what unit it will employ. It is thus useful to examine complex behaviour and to consider the usefulness of other units of analysis than the s–r unit. In exploring the analysis of behaviour by means of the TOTE unit – and possibly others not yet put forward – students of human development may discover the variables in the process.

References

ANNETT, J. (1969), *Feedback and Human Behaviour*, Penguin.

BANDURA, A., and WALTERS, R. H. (1963), *Social Learning and Personality Development*, Holt, Rinehart & Winston.

BARTLETT, F. C. (1932), *Remembering: A Study in Experimental and Social Psychology*, Cambridge University Press.

BARTLETT, F. C. (1958), *Thinking: An Experimental and Social Study*, Allen & Unwin.

BECKWITH, M., and RESTLE, F. (1966), 'Process of enumeration', *Psychol. Rev.*, vol. 73, pp. 437–44.

BELMONT, J. M., and BUTTERFIELD, E. C. (1969), 'The relations of short-term memory to development and intelligence', in H. W. Reese (ed.) *Advances in Child Development and Behaviour*, vol. 4, Academic Press.

BEM, S. L. (1970), 'The role of comprehension in children's problem solving', *Devel. Psychol.*, vol. 2, pp. 351–8.

BERLYNE, D. E. (1958), 'The influence of the albedo and complexity of stimuli on visual fixation in the human infant', *Brit. J. Psychol.*, vol. 49, pp. 315–18.

BERLYNE, D. E. (1960), *Conflict, Arousal and Curiosity*, McGraw-Hill.

BERLYNE, D. E. (1963), 'Motivational problems raised by exploratory and epistemic behavior', in S. Koch (ed.), *Psychology: A Study of a Science*, vol. 5, McGraw-Hill.

BERLYNE, D. E. (1965), *Structure and Direction in Thinking*, Wiley.

BOWER, T. G. R. (1967), 'The development of object permanence: some studies in existence constancy', *Percept. Psychophys.*, vol. 2, pp. 411–18.

BRACKBILL, Y., and FITZGERALD, H. E. (1969), 'Development of sensory analyzers during infancy', in H. W. Reese (ed.), *Advances in Child Development and Behavior*, vol. 4, Academic Press.

BRAINE, M. D. S. (1963), 'The ontogeny of English phrase structure: the first phase', *Language*, vol. 39, pp. 1–13.

BROWN, R., and FRASER, C. (1964), 'The acquisition of syntax', in U. Bellugi and R. Brown (eds.), *The Acquisition of Language*, Society for Research into Child Development, pp. 43–79.

BRUNER, J. S. (1964), 'The course of cognitive growth', *Amer. J. Psychol.*, vol. 19, pp. 1–15. Reprinted in P. C. Wason and P. N. Johnson-Laird (eds.), *Thinking and Reasoning*, Penguin, 1968.

BRUNER, J. S. et al. (1966), *Studies in Cognitive Growth*, Wiley.

BRUNER, J. S. (1966), 'On cognitive growth', in J. S. Bruner et al., *Studies in Cognitive Growth*, Wiley.

BRUNER, J. S. (1968), *Processes of Cognitive Growth: Infancy*, Clark University Press.

BRUNER, J. S., and BRUNER, B. M. (1968), 'On voluntary action and its hierarchical structure', *Int. J. Psychol.*, vol. 3, pp. 239–55.

BRUNER, J. S., GOODNOW, J. J., and AUSTIN, G. A. (1956), *A Study of Thinking*, Wiley.

BRUNER, J. S., and KENNEY, H. J. (1966), 'On multiple ordering', in J. S. Bruner et al., *Studies in Cognitive Growth*, Wiley.

BRUNSWIK, E. (1957), 'Scope and aspects of the cognitive problem', in *Contemporary Approaches to Cognition: The Colorado Symposium*, Harvard University Press.

CANTOR, J. H. (1965), 'Transfer of stimulus pretraining to motor paired-associate and discrimination learning tasks', in L. P. Lipsett and C. S. Spiker (eds.), *Advances in Child Development and Behavior*, vol. 2, Academic Press.

CORSINI, D. A., PICK, A. D., and FLAVELL, J. H. (1968), 'Production deficiency of non-verbal mediators in young children', *Child Devel.*, vol. 39, pp. 53–8.

DEUTSCH, J. A. (1960), *The Structural Basis of Behaviour*, Cambridge University Press.

DONALDSON, M. (1963), *A Study of Children's Thinking*, Tavistock.

DONALDSON, M., and BALFOUR, G. (1968), 'Less is more: a study of language comprehension in children', *Brit. J. Psychol.*, vol. 59, pp. 461–71.

ELKIND, D. (1961), 'The development of the additive composition of classes in the child: Piaget replication study III', *J. genet. Psychol.*, vol. 99, pp. 51–7.

FANTZ, R. L. (1963), 'Pattern vision in newborn infants', *Science*, vol. 140, pp. 296–7.

FLAVELL, J. H., BEACH, D. H., and CHINSKY, J. M. (1966), 'Spontaneous verbal rehearsal in a memory task as a function of age', *Child Devel.*, vol. 37, pp. 283–9.

FURTH, H. G. (1964), 'Research with the deaf: implications for language and cognition', *Psychol. Bull.*, vol. 62, pp. 145–64.

FURTH, H. G. (1968), 'Piaget's theory of knowledge: the nature of representation and interiorization', *Psychol. Rev.*, vol. 75, pp. 143–54.

GIBSON, E. J. (1969), *Principles of Perceptual Learning and Development*, Appleton-Century-Crofts.

GREENFIELD, P. M., REICH, C. H., and OLVER, R. R. (1966), 'On culture and equivalence: II', in J. S. Bruner et al., *Studies in Cognitive Growth*, Wiley.

GUNTHER, M. (1961), 'Infant behaviour at the breast', in B. M. Foss (ed.), *Determinants of Infant Behaviour*, vol. 1, Methuen.

HAITH, M. M. (1966), 'The response of the human newborn to visual movement', *J. exp. child Psychol.*, vol. 3, pp. 235–43.

HALVERSON, H. M. (1931), 'An experimental study of prehension in infants by means of systematic cinema records', *Genet. psychol. Monogr.*, vol. 10, pp. 107–286.

HARLOW, H. F. (1949), 'The formation of learning sets', *Psychol. Rev.*, vol. 56, pp. 51–65.

HARLOW, H. F. (1950), 'Analysis of discrimination learning by monkeys', *J. exp. Psychol.*, vol. 46, pp. 26–39.

HEBB, D. O. (1949), *The Organization of Behavior*, Wiley.

HEBB, D. O. (1960), 'The American revolution', *Amer. Psychol.*, vol. 15, pp. 735–45.

HEBB, D. O. (1966), *A Textbook of Psychology*, Saunders.

HEIDBREDER, E. F. (1928), 'Problem-solving in children and adults', *J. genet. Psychol.*, vol. 35, pp. 522–45.

HELD, R., and HEIN, A. (1963), 'Movement produced stimulation in the development of visually guided behavior', *J. comp. physiol. Psychol.*, vol. 56, pp. 872–6.

HULL, C. L. (1920), 'Quantitative aspects of the evolution of concepts', *Psychol. Monogr.*, vol. 28, no. 123.

HUMPHREY, G. (1951), *Thinking*, Methuen.

HUNTER, W. S., and BARTLETT, S. C. (1948), 'Double alternation behavior in young children', *J. exp. Psychol.*, vol. 38, pp. 558–67.

HUTT, C. (1967), 'Effects of stimulus novelty on manipulatory exploration in an infant', *J. child Psychol. Psychiat.*, vol. 8, pp. 241–7.

INHELDER, B., and PIAGET, J. (1958), *The Growth of Logical Thinking*, trans. A. Parsons and S. Milgram, Routledge & Kegan Paul.

INHELDER, B., and PIAGET, J. (1964), *The Early Growth of Logic in the Child*, trans. E. A. Lunzer and D. Papert, Routledge & Kegan Paul.

INHELDER, B., BOVET, M., SINCLAIR, H., and SMOCK, C. D. (1966), 'On cognitive development', *Amer. Psychol.*, vol. 21, pp. 160–64.

JACOBSON, E. (1930), 'Electrical measurements of neuromuscular states during mental activities: II. Imagination and recollection of various muscular acts', *Amer. J. Physiol.*, vol. 94, pp. 22–34.

JACOBSON, E. (1932), 'The electrophysiology of mental activities', *Amer. J. Psychol.*, vol. 44, pp. 677–94.

KENDLER, H. H., and KENDLER, T. S. (1962), 'Vertical and horizontal processes in problem-solving', *Psychol. Rev.*, vol. 69, pp. 1–16.

KENDLER, T. S. (1963), 'Development of mediating responses in children', in J. C. Wright and J. Kagan (eds.), *Basic Cognitive Processes in Children*, Society for Research in Child Development, pp. 33–48.

KENDLER, T. S., and KENDLER, H. H. (1959), 'Reversal and non-reversal shifts in kindergarten children', *J. exp. Psychol.*, vol. 58, pp. 56–60.

KENDLER, T. S., and KENDLER, H. H. (1967), 'Experimental analysis of inferential behavior in children', in L. P. Lipsett and C. S. Spiker (eds.), *Advances in Child Development and Behavior*, vol. 3, Academic Press.

KESSEN, W. (1967), 'Sucking and looking: two organized congenital patterns of behavior in the human newborn', in H. W. Stevenson, E. H. Hess and H. Rheingold (eds.), *Early Behavior: Comparative and Developmental Approaches*, Wiley.

KÖHLER, W. (1925), *The Mentality of Apes*, trans. E. Winter, Harcourt, Brace & World.

KUENNE, M. R. (1946), 'Experimental investigation of the relation of language to transposition behavior in young children', *J. exp. Psychol.*, vol. 36, pp. 471–90.

LASHLEY, K. S. (1951), 'The problem of serial order in behavior', in L. P. Jeffress (ed.), *Cerebral Mechanisms in Behavior: The Hixon Symposium*, Wiley. Reprinted in K. Pribram (ed.), *Brain and Behaviour*, vol. 2, Penguin, 1969.

LESKOW, S., and SMOCK, C. D. (1970), 'Developmental changes in problem-solving strategies', *Devel. Psychol.*, vol. 2, pp. 414–22.

LEVINE, M. (1959), 'A model of hypothesis behavior in discrimination learning set', *Psychol. Rev.*, vol. 66, pp. 353–66.

LEWIS, M. M. (1963), *Language, Thought and Personality in Infancy and Childhood*, Harrap.

LÉZINE, I., STAMBAK, M., and CASATI, I. (1969), *Les Etapes de l'Intelligence Sensori-Motrice*, Centre de Psychologie Appliquée.

LING, B. C. (1941), 'Form discrimination as a learning cue in infants', *Comp. Psychol. Monogr.*, vol. 17, no. 86.

LIPSITT, L. P. (1963), 'Learning in the first year of life', in L. P. Lipsett and C. S. Spiker (eds.), *Advances in Child Development and Behavior*, vol. 1, Academic Press.

LIPSITT, L. P. (1966), 'Can human newborns learn?', *Abst. Bull. Brit. Psychol. Soc.*, vol. 19, pp. 71–2.

LONG, L. (1940), 'Conceptual relationships in children: the concept of roundness', *J. genet. Psychol.*, vol. 57, pp. 289–315.

LOVELL, K. (1959), 'A follow-up study of some aspects of the work of Piaget and Inhelder on the child's conception of space', *Brit. J. educ. Psychol.*, vol. 29, pp. 104–17.

LOVELL, K. (1961), 'A follow-up study of Inhelder and Piaget's *The Growth of Logical Thinking*', *Brit. J. Psychol.*, vol. 52, pp. 143–53.

LOVELL, K., HEALEY, D., and ROWLAND, A. D. (1962), 'The growth of some geometrical concepts', *Child Devel.*, vol. 33, pp. 751–67.

LOVELL, K., and OGILVIE, E. (1960), 'A study of the concept of conservation of substance in the junior school child', *Brit. J. educ. Psychol.*, vol. 30, pp. 109–18.

LOVELL, K., and OGILVIE, E. (1961a), 'The growth of the concept of volume in junior school children', *J. child Psychol. Psychiat.*, vol. 2, pp. 118–26.

LOVELL, K., and OGILVIE, E. (1961b), 'A study of the conservation of weight in junior school children', *Brit. J. educ. Psychol.*, vol. 31, pp. 138–44.

LOVELL, K., and SLATER, A. (1960), 'The growth of the concept of time: a comparative study', *J. child Psychol. Psychiat.*, vol. 1, pp. 179–90.

LOVELL, K., MITCHELL, B., and EVERETT, I. R. (1962), 'An experimental study of the growth of some logical structures', *Brit. J. Psychol.*, vol. 53, pp. 175–88.

LUNZER, E. A. (1960), *Recent Studies in Britain Based on the Work of Jean Piaget*, National Foundation for Educational Research.

LUNZER, E. A. (1964), 'Translator's introduction' in B. Inhelder and J. Piaget, *The Early Growth of Logic in the Child*, Routledge & Kegan Paul.

LUNZER, E. A. (1968), *The Regulation of Behaviour: Development in Learning*, vol. 1, Staples Press.

LURIA, A. R. (1959), 'The directive function of speech in development and dissolution: part I', *Word*, vol. 15, pp. 341–52. Reprinted in R. C. Oldfield and J. C. Marshall (eds.), *Language*, Penguin, 1968.

LURIA, A. R. (1961), *The Role of Speech in the Regulation of Normal and Abnormal Behaviour*, Pergamon.

McCARTHY, D. (1954), 'Language development in children', in L. Carmichael (ed.), *Manual of Child Psychology*, Wiley.

MACCOBY, M., and MODIANO, N. (1966), 'On culture and equivalence: I', in J. S. Bruner *et al.*, *Studies in Cognitive Growth*, Wiley.

McLAUGHLIN, G. H. (1963), 'Psycho-logic: a possible alternative to Piaget's formulation', *Brit. J. educ. Psychol.*, vol. 33, pp. 61–7.

MILLER, G. A., GALANTER, E., and PRIBRAM, K. H. (1960), *Plans and the Structure of Behavior*, Holt, Rinehart & Winston.

MILLER, W., and ERVIN, S. (1964), 'The development of grammar in child language', in U. Bellugi and R. Brown (eds.), *The Acquisition of Language*, Society for Research in Child Development, pp. 9–34.

MOSHER, F. A., and HORNSBY, J. R. (1966), 'On asking questions', in J. S. Bruner *et al.*, *Studies in Cognitive Growth*, Wiley.

MUNN, N. L. (1961), *The Evolution and Growth of Human Behaviour*, Harrap.

NEISSER, U. (1967), *Cognitive Psychology*, Appleton-Century-Crofts.

OLSON, D. R. (1966), 'On conceptual strategies', in J. S. Bruner *et al.*, *Studies in Cognitive Growth*, Wiley.

OSGOOD, C. E. (1953), *Method and Theory in Experimental Psychology*, Oxford University Press.

PIAGET, J. (1951), *Play Dreams and Imitation in Childhood*, trans. C. Gattegno and F. M. Hodgson, Heinemann.

PIAGET, J. (1952), *The Child's Conception of Number*, trans. C. Gattegno and F. M. Hodgson, Routledge & Kegan Paul.

PIAGET, J. (1953), *The Origins of Intelligence in the Child*, trans. M. Cook, Routledge & Kegan Paul.

PIAGET, J. (1955), *The Construction of Reality in the Child*, trans. M. Cook, Routledge & Kegan Paul.

PIAGET, J. (1961), *Les Mécanismes Perceptifs*, Presses Universitaires de France.

PIAGET, J. (1968), *On the Development of Memory and Identity*, trans. E. Duckworth, Clark University Press.

PIAGET, J., and INHELDER, B. (1956), *The Child's Conception of Space*, trans. F. J. Langdon and J. L. Lunzer, Routledge & Kegan Paul.

PIAGET, J., and INHELDER, B. (1969a), 'Mental images', in P. Fraisse and J. Piaget (eds.), *Experimental Psychology: Its Scope and Method: VII. Intelligence*, trans. T. Surridge, Routledge & Kegan Paul.

PIAGET, J., and INHELDER, B. (1969b), 'Intellectual operations and their development', in P. Fraisse and J. Piaget (eds.), *Experimental Psychology: Its Scope and Method: VII. Intelligence*, trans. T. Surridge, Routledge & Kegan Paul.

PIAGET, J., INHELDER, B., and SZEMINSKA, A. (1960), *The Child's Conception of Geometry*, trans. E. A. Lunzer, Routledge & Kegan Paul.

POTTER, M. C. (1966), 'On perceptual recognition', in J. S. Bruner *et al. Studies in Cognitive Growth*, Wiley.

RAYNER, E. H. (1958), 'A study of evaluative problem-solving: II. Developmental observations', *Q. J. exp. Psychol.*, vol. 10, pp. 193–206.

REESE, H. W. (1962), 'Verbal mediation as a function of age level', *Psychol. Bull.*, vol. 59, pp. 502–9.

REESE, H. W. (1963), 'Discrimination learning set in children', in L. P. Lipsett and C. S. Spiker (eds.), *Advances in Child Development and Behavior*, vol. 1, Academic Press.

RHEINGOLD, H. L., GEWIRTZ, J. L., and ROSS, H. W. (1959), 'Social conditioning of vocalisations in the infant', *J. comp. physiol. Psychol.*, vol. 52, pp. 68–73.

SALTAPEK, P., and KESSEN, W. (1966), 'Visual scanning of triangles by the human newborn', *J. exp. child Psychol.*, vol. 3, pp. 155–67.

SCHAFFER, H. R., and EMERSON, P. E. (1964), *The Development of Social Attachments in Infancy*, Society for Research in Child Development.

SCHAFFER, H. R., and PARRY, M. H. (1969), 'Perceptual-motor behaviour in infancy as a function of age and stimulus similarity', *Brit. J. Psychol.*, vol. 60, pp. 1–9.

SEMB, G., and LIPSITT, L. P. (1968), 'The effects of acoustic stimulation on cessation and initiation of non-nutritive sucking in neonates', *J. exp. child Psychol.*, vol. 6, pp. 585–97.

SINCLAIR-DE-ZWART, H. (1969), 'Developmental psycholinguistics', in D. Elkind and J. H. Flavell (eds.), *Studies in Cognitive Development*, Oxford University Press.

SIQUELAND, E. R., and LIPSITT, L. P. (1966), 'Conditioned head-turning in human newborns', *J. exp. child Psychol.*, vol. 3, pp. 356–76.

SKINNER, B. F. (1938), *The Behavior of Organisms: An Experimental Analysis*, Appleton-Century-Crofts.

SKINNER, B. F. (1953), *Science and Human Behaviour*, Macmillan.

SOKOLOV, Y. N. (1963), *Perception and the Conditioned Reflex*, trans. S. W. Waydenfeld, Pergamon.

STAPLES, R. (1932), 'The responses of infants to color', *J. exp. Psychol.*, vol. 15, pp. 119–41.

TERMAN, L. M., and MERRILL, M. A. (1937), *Measuring Intelligence*, Harrap.

TINKLEPAUGH, O. L. (1928), 'An experimental study of representative factors in monkeys', *J. comp. physiol. Psychol.*, vol. 8, pp. 197–236.

VALENTINE, C. W. (1942), *The Psychology of Early Childhood*, Methuen.

VURPILLOT, E. (1968), 'The development of scanning strategies and their relation to visual differentiation', *J. exp. child Psychol.*, vol. 6, pp. 632–50.

VYGOTSKY, L. S. (1962), *Thought and Language*, trans. E. Hanfmann and G. Vakar, Wiley and MIT Press.

WEIR, R. H. (1962), *Language in the Crib*, Mouton.

WELCH, L. (1939a), 'The development of size discrimination between the ages of 12 and 40 months', *J. genet, Psychol.*, vol. 55, pp. 243–68.

WELCH, L. (1939b), 'The development and discrimination of form and area', *J. Psychol.*, vol. 7, pp. 37–54.

WETHERICK, N. E., and FREELAND, C. (1969), 'Inductive thinking in children of primary school age', *Brit. J. Psychol.*, vol. 60, pp. 11–16.

WHITE, B. L. (1969), 'The initial co-ordination of sensori-motor schemas in human infants: Piaget's ideas and the role of experience', in D. Elkind and J. H. Flavell (eds.), *Studies in Cognitive Development*, Oxford University Press.

WHITE, B. L., CASTLE, P., and HELD, R. (1964), 'Observations on the development of visually directed reaching', *Child Devel.*, vol. 35, pp. 349–64.

WHITE, S. H. (1965), 'Evidence for a hierarchical arrangement of learning processes', in L. P. Lipsett and C. S. Spiker (eds.), *Advances in Child Development and Behavior*, vol. 2, Academic Press.

WOHLWILL, J. F. (1960), 'Developmental studies of perception', *Psychol. Bull.*, vol. 57, pp. 249–88.

WOLFF, P. (1963), 'Observations on the early development of smiling', in B. M. Foss (ed.), *Determinants of Infant Behaviour*, vol. 2, Methuen.

WOLFF, P. (1966), 'The causes, controls and organization of behavior in the neonate', *Psychol. Issues*, vol. 5, no. 1.

WOODWARD, W. M. (1959), 'The behaviour of idiots interpreted by Piaget's theory of sensori-motor development', *Brit. J. educ. Psychol.*, vol. 29, pp. 60–71.

WOODWARD, W. M. (1960), 'Early experiences and later social responses of severely subnormal children', *Brit. J. med. Psychol.*, vol. 33, pp. 123–32.

WOODWARD, W. M. (1961), 'Concepts of number in the mentally subnormal studied by Piaget's method', *J. child Psychol. Psychiat.*, vol. 2, pp. 249–59.

WOODWARD, W. M. (1962a), 'Concepts of space in the mentally subnormal studied by Piaget's method', *Brit. J. soc. clin. Psychol.*, vol. 1, pp. 25–37.

WOODWARD, W. M. (1962b), 'The application of Piaget's theory to the training of the subnormal', *J. ment. Subnorm.*, vol. 8, pp. 3–11.

WOODWARD, W. M. (1963), 'Early experiences and behaviour disorders in severely subnormal children', *Brit. J. soc. clin. Psychol.*, vol. 2, pp. 174–84.

Index